# The Deep Limitless Air

# The Deep Limitless Air

*A Memoir in Pieces*

## Mary Allen

BLUE LIGHT PRESS ◆ 1ST WORLD PUBLISHING

SAN FRANCISCO ◆ FAIRFIELD ◆ DELHI

*The Deep Limitless Air*
*A Memoir in Pieces*
Copyright ©2022 Mary Allen

BLUE LIGHT PRESS
www.bluelightpress.com
bluelightpress@aol.com

1ST WORLD PUBLISHING
PO Box 2211
Fairfield, IA 52556
www.1stworldpublishing.com

BOOK & COVER DESIGN
Melanie Gendron
melaniegendron999@gmail.com

COVER PHOTO
Mary Allen

AUTHOR PHOTO
Dan Coffey

FIRST EDITION

Library of Congress Cataloging-in-Publication Data

ISBN: 978-1-4218-3715-4

# Praise for *The Rooms of Heaven*

"Allen's hypnotic memoir is sad, mysterious and beautiful." *Booklist*

"Wrenching in its spare, humble prose." *Esquire*

"Engrossing but never self-indulgent or sensationalist." *Kirkus Reviews*

"Remarkably lucid and dream-like, *The Rooms of Heaven* will probably fill your imagination for a long time after you have left its pages." *Detroit Free Press*

"Extraordinary not only in its candor, but in the way it lures you in." Newsweek

"Intelligent, humorous, unsentimental…[The Rooms of Heaven] convinces us that the mystery of love is indeed far greater than and more profound than the mystery of death." Francine Prose, *Elle*

"This book may haunt your imagination. Mary Allen raises many questions—about the nature of love, the meaning of death, the possibility of a world beyond this one—in remarkably lucid, sometimes shimmering prose. I was seduced into reading it by the opening, one of the most evocative passages about the Midwest I've ever read. Then I kept reading, and couldn't stop until I was done." Susan Allen Toth, author of *Blooming: A Small Town Girlhood*

"A memoir unlike any I've read—a page turner told in spare, elegant prose…. A profoundly moving story about the mortality of man and the immortality of love." Jo Ann Beard, author of *The Boys of My Youth*

"I know of no other writer with the gifts to take the trappings of contemporary tragedy and spin from them such a bewitching and convincing tale of the redemptive magic of everyday love. Mary Allen writes with the music of a waltz, and with the vulnerable irony of a ballad—pitch perfect, singular, and bittersweet." Honor Moore, author of *The Bishop's Daughter* and *Our Revolution, A Mother and Daughter at Midcentury*

"The Rooms of Heaven shows the unexpected ways in which our lives can be transformed." Lucy Grealy, author of *Autobiography of a Face*

In memory of my sister, Christine Allen

# Bees

The bees arrived at the post office in Easthampton early this morning. Someone called my father from the post office at eight a.m. and told him in no uncertain terms to get over there right away and pick them up. My father has already assembled the hive in a spot under some trees in his backyard, and now he and I are going to his house to install the bees in it.

"When I got to the post office the guy was all shook up," my father tells me as we putter along Route 66 to Westhampton. "He said, 'Get these goddamn things out of here.'" He mimics the postal worker's anxious irritated tone of voice with an air of amusement, as if there's something craven about being afraid of 25,000 bees buzzing angrily inside a plywood box.

It's my sophomore year of college and I'm taking a bee-keeping class for a science requirement. The teacher played us a movie about the social life of the hive. It showed the male bees, called drones, flying high up into the air trying to mate with the queen and then, their sole function having been fulfilled, being kicked out by the worker bees in the autumn so they didn't use up precious space and food over the winter. The drones fought for their lives as they were being ejected from the hive, battling with the worker bees and doing the bee equivalent of digging in their heels and clinging to the edges of the doorway while the workers calmly and persistently shoved them out, from which I concluded that insects fear death but lack compassion.

The instructor also explained how the queen is created by the worker bees lavishing certain larvae with royal jelly; how the worker bees, which are essentially stunted neutered females, retain their reproductive equipment and can squeeze out an emergency egg if the queen dies; how, incredibly, when a 'scout' bee discovers a good source of nectar or pollen she goes back to the hive and performs a unique set of movements, called a waggle dance, which lets the other bees know the distance and direction of the food; how bees are not actually busy but spend much of their time wandering around the hive "resting and patrolling."

The instructor also taught us how to set up and maintain a working beehive, and he made it possible for those of us who wanted to, to acquire what we needed to start our own hives—told us where to buy the makings of the beehive and how to construct it and made arrangements for us to order a box of 25,000 worker bees and one queen for $25.

It's the 1970s and I've read the *Whole Earth Catalogue*; I have fantasies of being able to live off the land, to grow my own vegetables and milk my own cows and eat eggs from chickens that scratch in the dirt in front of my house, and I think having a beehive would be a good place to start. The only problems is, I live in an apartment in Northampton where there's no yard for chickens or even space for a garden and where there's certainly no place where I can keep bees. But my father lives in the country and has space for a beehive and he too is enthusiastic about the idea of living off the land; he always wanted to be a farmer and it isn't much of a leap from that to embracing the back-to-nature movement of the 1960s and '70s, which is still happening in this moment although it's waning. Toward the end of the beekeeping class I called him and told him that we could get the makings of a beehive and the bees themselves for very little money and that I had all the information we'd need to know what to do with them, and I asked him whether he'd like to go in on that project with me, installing and keeping the beehive behind his house. He said that he would love to. In fact, he was even more excited about the idea than I was. And so we ordered the bees and the makings of the hive and now we're ready to become beekeepers.

The thought of setting up a beehive in my father's yard while my mother's inside the house knowing I'm there makes me unbelievably anxious, and deep inside I know I can't help my father maintain the hive over time the way he and I have been saying I will. I'm afraid of my mother, for reasons too complicated to explain and which I don't even really understand myself yet. All I know is that my fear goes well beyond any normal everyday experiences, arises out of my mother's mental illness during my early childhood and beyond, and is the central fact of my life. That she 'rejected' me as a little girl, as my father told me—many years later I'll realize she must've had postpartum depression or possibly psychosis after I was born. That because I was so afraid of her I lived with a foster family down the road, the Paysons, for most of my childhood, which made my mother even angrier. That I clung to my home in the Paysons' house like one of those drones resisting leaving the hive, although my mother tried to make me live at home and even the Paysons might not have been happy to have me by the time I got into my teens. That I lived with my mother and father for three weeks after I turned eighteen, then ran away in the middle of dinner when my mother was yelling at me and I never went back.

Seeing my mother, or, more importantly, being seen by her, has come to seem dangerous, unthinkable, out of proportion to reality. I think I can probably stand to go to the house this once and help my father install the bees in the hive but no more than that. And even that thought is taking place on some subterranean level I'm not very conscious of. Mostly I'm just ignoring the reality of the situation, the way I ignore so many things in my life right now.

My father drives slowly to Westhampton, past the woods and over the bridges and up the hills and around the curves I've been passing in cars driven by my father or the Paysons and in recent years by myself, for all my life. My father's house finally comes into view and he pulls into his driveway.

The bees are inside, he says. "You can go back and look at the hive while I go in and get them."

Feeling anxious and exposed, I make my way along the east side of the house, under the locust trees and past the picnic table and the windows of my sister's old bedroom. I feel like my mother is watching me, although I know that's something she would never do. But even though she won't be looking out the window, she'll know that I'm here, not because she has supernatural abilities but because my father will have told her, in his stubbornly naive refusal to understand that I wouldn't want her to know I was coming and at what time.

I stand by the beehive waiting for my father. It's a chilly gray Saturday at the end of March and I'm wearing a plaid wool coat with a sheepskin lining and a rim of sheepskin on the collar and the cuffs. It seems too late in the year to be wearing such a heavy coat but I would be cold without it today and it's thick enough to protect me from the bees. All of our bee-keeping equipment is assembled and sitting on the ground beside the hive where my father has left it. There's a hat with a net to put over your face and a smoker that you light a little fire inside and squeeze like a bellows to create a cloud of smoke. Those of us in the class who are getting bees are supposed to assemble all our own equipment, but my father has done most of that himself without my assistance, ordering the parts of the hive from a catalogue along with the directions for assembling them and purchasing the smoker and the net from the same place.

The bees had to be ordered and paid for through my teacher and I did that earlier, and in the sheepskin-lined pocket of my coat I have matches and paper for lighting the fire in the smoker. I've also brought a large ziplock bag full of sugar syrup which I prepared at home along with a round brown pollen patty made of ingredients I was told how to combine by the instructor. Once the bees are in the hive you're supposed to make a slit in the bag of sugar syrup with a razor blade and place it and the pollen patty on top of the inner workings of the hive so the bees will have something to eat right away. I've also brought a plastic spray bottle full of the same sugar syrup, which we're supposed to spray on the bees before we let them out of the box and which, along with puffing them with smoke from the smoker, will keep them from flying away or stinging us while we dump them into the hive. The sugar syrup makes their wings heavy so they can't fly and the smoke acts like a kind of drug that makes them tired.

After a few long minutes while I wait for my father to come out of the house—I imagine him standing in the kitchen talking to my mother, her asking him questions about me and him answering—I see him coming back along the side of the house, carefully holding out a rectangular plywood box between his hands.

He places the box—an angry buzzing noise is coming from it—on the ground near the hive. "Are we ready?" he says, and I nod. He takes a screwdriver out of his back pocket and uses it to pry the lid off the top of the box. Inside, lying in a nest of straw, is a slightly smaller box made of heavy black metal mesh. Wearing gloves, my father carefully removes that box from the plywood box and lays it on the ground and we both stare down it. There are some tiny bee parts, legs and wings, protruding through the holes in the mesh and I can see that they're attached to the corpses of some squished bees and I can sense the presence of a mass of writhing squirming humming bees inside the box.

"Now for the most important part," my father says, fishing around in the straw. He pulls out yet another box, this one small, narrow, and rectangular, about the size of a matchbox. There's a tiny circular hole in the top covered by a fine mesh screen and my father holds the box to his right eye and peers through the hole to see if the box's contents—the precious queen—is still alive. If she's dead we'll have to rush to get a new queen and no matter what we do there's a good chance a new queen won't make it on time and the hive won't survive. My father nods, then hands me the little box, and when I look inside I see the queen, her long body—she's at least ten times the size of a regular worker bee—taking up most of the space. Her stinger pulses and her legs move slowly and her pointy-faced head shifts slightly from side to side, as if she's testing the limits of her confinement.

I don the beekeeper hat with its face net and tie its strings under my chin—my father and I have agreed beforehand that I'll wear the hat since he's not as afraid as I am of getting stung. I hand my father the matches and he lights a little fire in the smoker and starts opening and closing its bellows, blowing smoke toward the bees in the box. At the same time I give them several hefty squirts from the sugar syrup bottle. They buzz angrily, but it seems to me there's a new, slightly soporific tone to their buzzing and I think I can see just a little less movement inside their box. My father and I nod at each other. The time has come to open the box holding the 25,000 bees—the queen will stay in her tiny cage a little longer—and let them out. The plan is to hold them over the hive and dump them in, onto the frames, then place the pollen patty and the ziplock bag of sugar syrup on top of the frames and cover the hive with its pre-made cover.

My father rests the bee-containing box on top of the hive. It has a door with a twisted wire latch and my father turns the latch to the right and pulls the door open.  Immediately some bees fly out, just a few at first, then a few more and then more. My father holds the box above the hive and tries to shake the remaining bees onto the frames in the hive and about half the bees go where they're supposed to go. About three-quarters of those bees stay put and begin walking busily around investigating their new home.  But a quarter of the bees that landed on the hive fly up in the air and join the other bees that flew out of the box instead of going in the hive and all of them together begin to swarm around my father and me.

I look down at my arm and see that two have landed on the sleeve of my coat near my elbow. I feel a stab of fear but I don't know what to do, so I decide to just ignore the bees on my coat and continue going through the motions of installing the bees in the hive, doing the things they taught us to do in the class. Then I feel a bee land on my hand and then another one land next to it and then I notice that a third bee is crawling up my wrist and then I see it and another bee disappear inside the sleeve of my coat. Again I try to ignore that because I don't know what else to do, because I don't know how to stop it from happening.  Then I feel the piercing needle of a bee-sting on my back, then I feel another one, then there's one on my arm.  I'm filled with a terrible panic and I run away from the hive, tearing off my coat.  I throw my coat down on the ground and take my shirt off and run even farther from the hive.  I picture myself with hundreds, thousands, of bees all over me, stinging me everywhere.  But I don't get any more stings—some of the sugar syrup I sprayed on the bees must've gotten on my coat, I realize, and now that the coat is gone the bees aren't that interested in me anymore.

I stop running about fifty feet from the hive and stand there panting. I wait for more bees to find me but none do and I begin to calm down, although the bee stings on my back and arms—there's one on my neck too—are pulsing and throbbing with their fierce poisonous pain.

"Can you hear me?" I yell to my father, who's still standing fearlessly, hatless, netless, among the swarm of bees next to the hive.

"Yeah," he shouts back to me. "Tell me what to do."

So standing there, still wearing the bee hat with the net over my face and with a bra on but no shirt, I shout out directions for continuing to install the hive: "Now you put the pollen patty on top. Now you slit the bag of sugar syrup." It's hard to yell loud enough, to remember what my father's supposed to do and tell him in enough detail. He keeps shouting, "What?" and then I have to yell the directions all over again. It's sort of like those moments in dreams where you're trying to make yourself heard or running away for all you're worth but no sound will come out or you can't get anywhere. The most delicate procedure is introducing the queen into the hive. It's impossible to convey all the precautions we were told in class—make sure the queen doesn't fly away, make sure she appears to be acclimated after you place her in the hive and blah blah blah—so I just give up and let my father try to do it on his own.

Despite that and everything else, the bees get installed in the hive. A few have been lost but for the most part they seem to be getting along okay, my father tells me, approaching me across the lawn when the job is done. "I didn't even get stung once," he says proudly. "And you had on the hat with the net."

I've put my shirt back on by now and under it my stings are throbbing more and more violently. I begin to feel swollen and lightheaded. The thought that I could be having an allergic reaction intrudes on me and fills me with renewed panic. The fear makes my breath come shallowly, which seems like more evidence that I'm having an allergic reaction, and that makes me even more anxious.

"I think I might be having an allergic reaction," I tell my father.

"Do you have a problem with bee stings?" he says, looking worried.

"I don't know," I say. "I think I might have had a reaction the last time I got stung. I've heard the allergy gets worse every time."

"I'll take you to Northampton right now," my father says, "and if it doesn't go away we'll go to the emergency room."

We walk quickly to the car and get in and my father backs out of the driveway and drives away. I don't even think about my mother in that moment—I don't think about the fact that I haven't seen her or wonder whether she was looking out the window when I was in the yard—and as my father and I get a couple of miles away from the house, I begin to breathe a little more easily and the itching and swelling, the panic and nervousness, begin to subside. Which is a good thing, because if it was real allergic reaction I would have been dead by now, or soon.

My father's beehive did well; the bees flourished and made honey. My father harvested a few bottles of it that year and more the following year. He put in a second hive; he bought a huge honey extractor and kept it in the room that used to be my sister's and sometimes my bedroom.

Eventually a bear lumbered out of the woods into my father's backyard and knocked over both hives and ate the honey and drove the bees away and my father decided not to replace them. I'm not sure why he made that decision, because as far as I know he loved being a beekeeper, loved puttering around with the hive, loved collecting the dripping honeycombs and extracting the sticky mess using the huge centrifugal-force-creating extractor in the middle of the floor in the spare bedroom, loved bottling the honey, more and more of it coming every year, and giving it away. He even loved the bees themselves. He called them girls—"the girls have been very busy today, the girls have been all over the clover on the lawn," he told me whenever we talked on the phone. He said they weren't afraid of him because he wasn't afraid of them and he claimed they never stung him.

But I never went near them again.

# Birthday Cake

"I hope it's just a false alarm!" my sister trills as the hot water pours over her on the other side of the shower curtain. I'm sitting on the edge of the bathtub in case she slips and falls. She's nine-and-a-half months pregnant and has been having what surely must be labor pains for about four hours. If she's going to have the baby now, she tells me, not for the first time, she doesn't want to go to the hospital before midnight because the hospital will charge her for another day. Her insurance won't cover the birth because she's a single mother.

It's February 18, 1973, she's twenty-one and I'm nineteen, and she's been living with me and my boyfriend in this Northampton apartment since the middle of December. Before that she lived with my parents and managed to conceal her pregnancy from my mother by wearing baggy shirts. She's always had a more normal mother-daughter connection with my mother than I do, but she's afraid my mother will disapprove of her pregnancy and freak out, plus my mother's started drinking day and night and Christine doesn't want her baby to be exposed to that. After she had been living with me for a couple of weeks my mother called one night and when I answered the phone she said, "Which one of you girls is pregnant?" Somebody had sent her a card that said congratulations you're going to be a grandmother. Sometimes I wonder now, all these years later, if it might have been my father, getting sick of all the subterfuge and tiptoeing around, who sent that card.

"It's Christine," I said to my mother, my voice tight with anxiety, and handed my sister the phone.

Christine and I chat companionably as she gets out of the shower and starts pulling on clothes. It's a little crowded in the bathroom but I don't want to leave her alone. Eventually she goes into the kitchen, stands at the counter, and starts mixing flour, sugar, and eggs together in a tan ceramic bowl with a stripe around the rim, then pours the batter into three round cake tins. While the cakes are baking she combines sugar and cocoa and butter in a smaller bowl and beats them into frosting with a handheld egg beater, and twenty minutes later she takes the round yellow cakes out of the oven, sticks a toothpick into each one, and pronounces them done.

It doesn't occur to me to ask her why she's doing this. She probably wouldn't tell me anyway, and my mind wanders to other things: how warm it is in the kitchen, how cold it is outside, the frost on the inside of the kitchen window, what my boyfriend Charlie is watching on TV in the other room. Every now and then Christine bends forward and winces—she's not keeping track of how often that's happening and neither am I. But it seems like it's happening more now than it was when she started baking.

While the yellow cakes are cooling on racks on the table she goes into her bedroom and comes out ten minutes later wearing warmer clothes: a pair of heavy dark-blue pregnancy sweatpants, a ribbed turtleneck sweater, and one of the long thick shirts she wore to conceal her pregnancy from our mother. She runs her hand over the tops of the cakes and decides they're cool enough, spreads a layer of frosting over each, stacks them one on top of the other, and covers the whole cake with more frosting.

"I don't feel too good," she says. "But I'm still not going to the hospital because it isn't midnight yet."

I look at the clock on the stove. It's 10:23.

By five past eleven she's shivering and moaning. We put on our coats and she wraps a blanket around her shoulders and we go out into the dark bitter-cold night and get in my red VW bug. The windshield's covered with frost and the car will not heat up. I keep having to grab a corner of Christine's blanket and wipe a clear circle on the windshield as we putt putt putt toward the hospital a mile or two away. Christine keeps shivering violently and I keep asking her nervously if she's cold.

Someone meets us outside the ER with a wheelchair but Christine insists on walking through the entrance on her own. I follow her to the elevator and she and I and an ER worker ride together to the maternity ward on the fourth floor. The ward consists of a labor room on one end of a long hallway and a delivery room on other end, with four chairs in a row between them for a waiting room. I sit down in one of the chairs and prepare to be there for the long haul. I hear someone screaming horribly in the labor room and I dread listening to my sister do that.

And then, one moment after I have that thought, the door to the labor room flies open and someone in scrubs wheels my sister past me on a stretcher. They disappear through the delivery room door and just a few minutes later I hear a tiny mewling cry like the sound of a kitten. A nurse appears briefly in the delivery room doorway. Congratulations, it's a girl, she says. A few minutes later another person holds the baby up to a square window to show her to me as if I'm the proud father. The baby is beautiful: intelligent open eyes, brown hair, perfect little features, not even red faced and wrinkly, as if she slipped right out and it wasn't stressful at all.

A while later I get to visit my sister in a room down the hall where they've taken her. She's tucked up in a bed holding the baby in the crook of her arm. The baby is wide awake, looking out through her deep blue eyes at this new world she finds herself in.  My sister is flushed and smiling; I've never seen her look so peaceful and pretty and happy.  A handsome doctor in green scrubs is standing beside her bed as if he doesn't want to leave.

"Go down to the car and get the cake," my sister says to me.

In the rush and anxiety of taking her to the hospital I somehow missed the fact that she brought the cake, but there it is, sitting on the backseat of my red VW as if awaiting its part on this night.  I move the car from where I left it outside the ER to a spot in the regular parking lot, then collect the cake, all three frosted layers of it, and carry it into the hospital. And then I can't remember where the maternity ward is.  It's one o'clock in the morning by now and no one's around.  I rush up and down deserted hallways on the second and third floor, carrying the cake, feeling embarrassed and frantic.  I finally run into a nurse who looks at me strangely.  "Can I help you?"

I explain the situation and she tells me how to get to the maternity ward, one flight up and to the right of the elevator. I find my sister in the room with the baby.  The doctor is still here and so is a nurse.  The nurse goes off to scrounge up a knife and some plastic forks and paper plates from the nurses' station and when she comes back my sister cuts the cake and we all stand around her bed eating a piece of it.  Christine eats some too: her daughter's first birthday cake.  It's moist and yellow and not too sweet, covered with creamy chocolate frosting with a hint of nuttiness—everything a good cake should be.


This morning when I was decluttering a corner of my desk I came across two photos of my sister.  I didn't know they were there, lurking among the Elmer's glue and dusty boxes of staples and pencils, and it was startling to see them, they practically jumped out at me.  *Here she is*—my sister grinning into the camera in one of them; mouth open, head flung back in a laugh in the other, wearing a red jacket with a shell necklace and black scarf, short white hair, earrings, glasses. I think someone must've given those pictures out at her memorial service and when I got home to Iowa City I squirreled them away behind that stuff on my desk, finding them painful to look at it. They're still surprisingly painful, not really because I've forgotten my sister is dead and they make me remember but because my sister is so bright and present in them, her her-ness, her is-ness, blaring out of those pictures so loudly it's almost as if she herself has stepped into the room. But she hasn't stepped into the room, she'll never be in the room again. What happened to that brightness, I wonder now, the same thing I've been wondering since my fiancé died almost thirty years ago. I feel sure that brightness must be somewhere.

I keep thinking about something I should have said at her memorial service. She died three days after Christmas a few years ago, and somebody, maybe Christine herself, who probably planned the whole thing with her friend who lived down the street, decided the service would be held in June that year so nobody would have to travel in the winter to get there. At the memorial, held in a public building not far from my sister's house in Williamsburg, Mass., I stood up at the podium in front of that roomful of people, all those friendly faces who knew her in one way or the other, and talked about the birth of her daughter. Most of the food was eaten by then, the remains pooling in the bottoms of bowls, pushed to the edges of plates and platters, crumbs and blobs and spills littering the white tablecloth, all that potluck food, tons of food, set out on four long tables arranged in a square: shrimp and meatballs and couscous and cookies, salads and fruit and casseroles and cupcakes, every bit of it as delicious and tastefully arranged as anything my sister herself would have made and brought. And now we're all sitting in an adjoining room, with people getting up spontaneously to say something, I've gotten up to say something.

I look out and see Jo Ann sitting in the middle of the second row—Jo Ann, my old friend who drove me here from upstate New York out of the kindness of her heart; I flew into Albany and am staying at her house. She'll drive us back there at the end of this day and three days from now she'll take me back to Albany. While we're waiting for the time to check-in for my flight we'll have dinner in a cavernous, overly air-conditioned, half-empty restaurant, where there won't be much on the menu that either of us can eat—a moment that sticks in my mind because of its singular bleakness—and after I leave, Jo Ann, in another amazing act of friendship, will box up and ship to me a huge pile of family photos and memorabilia from my sister's basement, which someone brought to the memorial service for me to take home.

I look out at her in the audience now and see that her mouth is twisted into a grimace and she's on the brink of tears, and that's when I almost lose it. But I don't. Instead I take a deep breath and tell the story of the cold winter night, the Volkswagen beetle with no heat, the cake, the birth of her daughter five minutes after we arrived in the hospital. And then I look over at my sister's daughter, forty-something now, wearing a sleeveless pink dress, standing behind me to my left, and say, "You were everything to her."

But what I didn't say, what I wish now that I had said, was, "My sister made everything look easy. She made giving birth look easy. She made being a single mother look easy." She even, I wouldn't have said even if I had said all the rest, made having ALS look easy. A few minutes from now her daughter will get up and talk about how Christine giggled on the phone when she talked about all the stuff she couldn't do, as if having a horrible progressive illness was funny, and a little while after that somebody will get up and say that my sister was in an ALS support group with her uncle and he said she put everybody in a good mood at the meetings. I believe it. She even made dying look easy, arranging her own death herself, choosing the date and time, facing it calmly and squarely with more grace and courage than I or anyone else could have done in a million years.

Was she faking it? Doing all that easy-making for others, suppressing the hard stuff so she wouldn't upset anyone around her, so she wouldn't feel the pain of it herself? Probably. But then I think of her being a single mother. I *know* that was easy for her and she didn't make it look easy for somebody else. She took her baby daughter with her everywhere, to work, to the grocery store, to softball games where she sat on a blanket on the grass on summer evenings and watched her married boyfriend play while his wife and his other two, "legitimate" daughters sat on their own blanket a few yards away. They're all here too, at her memorial service, her daughter's father in a wheelchair—he'll be dead himself in a matter of months—his wife and his two other grown-up daughters seated at the end of a row.

That was another thing Christine managed to do that nobody else could have done. She carried on a relationship with that married man for years, until it petered out when her daughter was about ten—his wife called her at one point toward the end and snapped out, "If you want him you can have him," and Christine said, in a high trilling nervous voice, "No thank you!" But for a long time she made it work, forged ahead as if none of the things that always matter in situations like that did matter, as if she wasn't living in a small town full of gossiping people who were talking about her, as if the wife wasn't jealous of her and she wasn't jealous of the wife, as if she was fine with being the other woman, a single woman who got crumbs from the guy instead of a whole meal—she had other relationships with other men at the same time, she made her own meal. And because that's what she did and how she looked at it, everybody else came to see it that way too. Everybody got used it. She turned the exceptional and the scandalous into a regular humdrum fact of life.

She named her daughter Leonika, after a friend. Leonika was a cute wispy-haired, round-eyed baby who learned how to kiss before she spoke her first word. She looked you straight in the eye, pursed her lips in a little O and sent out a kiss like a tiny soap bubble to everyone she encountered, me, her mother, the landlord, strangers in the grocery store. And also, I'm sure, although I wasn't there to see it, to *my* mother.

My poor mother, estranged from one daughter and avoided by the other, who had to hear about that daughter's pregnancy from an anonymous card, took instantly to Leonika and Leonika took instantly to her. My mother, who had always been so terrifying to me, who was really a stranger to me, whose descent into alcoholism resulted in DTs so bad she had to be hospitalized not long before Leonika was born, was regarded as a huggable, gift-giving, primary love object by her granddaughter. Leonika took my mother in with her straightforward gaze, pronounced her *Grandma* as soon as she could say it, and loved her with a fierce protectiveness. I heard about their burgeoning relationship from my sister, and my mother talked incessantly about Leonika, when I started being around my mother—how smart and strong Leonika was, how confident and self-assured. "She's going to be president someday," my mother said once, during the second or third time I was in my mother's presence after an eight-year hiatus. "There will be no stopping her."

It was true, what my mother said about Leonika. Once I heard Leonika say, in her shrill shrieking little voice when she was about five, to a country guy who lived down the road—at that time she and my sister still lived in the house we called the camp—"Mr. Dewey, do you shoot cats?" I was babysitting for her; we had taken a walk and run into Mr. Dewey by his mailbox. We could see his house from the road, a rundown shack set far back under some trees, wood smoke billowing from the chimney, a giant pile of stacked wood in the yard.

I have no idea how Leonika had heard that Mr. Dewey was a cat shooter. I barely knew who he was, only that he was one of those country people who live on the margins of society and was rumored to have a still. She just knew that about him, the way she knew other things she couldn't know, like how to get places; in a pinch my sister would ask her directions and she always somehow knew which way to go.

He ignored her and continued leafing through the stack of junk mail he'd found in his mailbox.

"Mr. Dewey!" she said again, more loudly and shrilly. "Do you shoot cats?" She had a baby-talk-leftover lisp, a way of mixing her *sh*s with *th*s, so it sounded like she was saying do you *thoot* cats. But her meaning was clear. Mr. Dewey continued to ignore her and she stared at him disapprovingly from the level of his pants legs. "Mr. Dewey!" she shrieked. "Do you shoot cats?"

It was obvious that he was not going to answer her. But then, just as I reached out to drag her away, he glanced down at her and said, "Ayah, I guess I do."


Sometime toward the end of her life, my sister had her bathroom redone. She still had speech at that point although it was slurred, she could still get around with a cane. But it was clear to her and everyone else that she wasn't going to be living in her house or any house much longer.

I visited her twice during the roughly two years between her diagnosis and death, and the first time I went I heard noises coming from the bathroom, went to the hallway and saw, through the open bathroom door, a chubby woman in paint-spattered overalls scraping wallpaper off the bathroom wall.

"Who's that?" I asked, back in the living room.

"That's Maureen," Christine said. "I'm paying her to renovate the bathroom. I never liked that bathroom!"

Christine had lived in that house for many years by then. She and her daughter moved there from the camp, which belonged to Christine's friend's parents, when Leonika was six; Leonika's father bought the house for them. Christine lived in that house for so long I find it hard to imagine she isn't still there; I even find it hard to picture the bathroom being any way other than how it always was, with flower-pattern wallpaper and a round mirror above a long fake-marble counter. The toilet was at the far end next to a window, with a ceiling-high shelf discretely separating the sight of the toilet from the rest of the room.

There were many problems involving water in that house. Once when one of us happened to go into the spare bedroom to get something on Christmas day, they found the radiator hissing loudly and spewing water all over the hardwood floor, which was never the same. And for a couple of years there was hot water in the toilet. No one knew about that either, for a while. It was just a slightly strange, somewhat unpleasant sensation wafting up from below as you were sitting there fiddling with the toilet paper roll, looking out the window. At least that's how I remember it. Eventually Christine came to terms with the fact that the toilet water was hot and got a plumber to fix whatever was causing it—it took a while for the guy to figure it out, she said.

Only my sister would have hot water in her toilet, I used to say to people. I didn't try to explain what I meant or even exactly know myself, but I knew it was true. Her life was filled with small wacky disasters, out-of-control details, unexplainable phenomena. I thought she loved it that way. I thought she created it all, accepted it all herself. It never occurred to me that she wanted to change things, that she would want to do something over at the last minute.

# Cockroaches

It's February 8, 1978, the day after the second biggest snow-storm in Boston history, and I'm sitting on a bench on Boston Common. There are towers of snow on all the benches and tree branches; I had to brush off the bench with my mitten to be able to sit down here. I took the Peter Pan bus from Northampton to the bus station on Tremont Street, walked to the subway station nearby and took the Green line to Park Street station, the underground trolley screeching and lurching and stinking of creosote, exactly like it did when I came to Boston to spend the week with my mother when I was three years old.

I sit here on this bench and wait till two-thirty, when I have an interview for a job, secretary to the product manager in the college division of Little, Brown and Company. I don't really know whether I want this job. If I get it I'll take it because that's what I do in my life at this time, just banging into the first thing and being sent to the next thing and bouncing off that to the next thing, like a ball in a pinball machine. But I'm not thinking I will get that job in this moment. I'm not thinking I won't get it either. I'm just here because a couple of weeks ago when I was in Boston with my friend Ron, I filled out an application for employment, any employment, at Little, Brown, thinking they would never call me. But someone from the personnel office did call me and it didn't even occur to me to say I wasn't interested in being secretary to the product manager in the college division. I just found out what time the interview was, took the bus, and here I am.

The sun is shining and the snow is sparkling and blobs of snow are falling off the trees nearby. The only other people around are two old Italian men sitting on a bench to my right, wearing mufflers and boots and porkpie hats. They're talking about the big snowstorm. "You know," one of them says to the other in a heavy Italian accent, "ever since they put a man on the moon, things just aren't the same. They put a hole in the atmosphere."


I'm pacing the floor of my apartment in Orient Heights in East Boston, talking on the telephone. For my first two weeks after getting the job at Little, Brown I stayed with my friend Beatrice and her husband and little boy in their apartment in Allston. I worked with Beatrice in my last job, as a clerk in the transcripts department at UMass in Amherst. She has lovely glossy black skin and a deep cheerful laugh. She talks about her village in Zaire, about her husband Hank, a skinny white guy with glasses that she met when he was in the Peace Corps; whenever something difficult happens she says *Oh life!* in a way that makes everything seem like it's going to be okay. She and Hank moved to Boston a few months ago, and when I got the job at Little, Brown I called her and she said that of course I should stay with them in their apartment, sleeping on the couch in the living room, until I found a place to live. Then a friend at her current job said *her* friend had a nice apartment in Orient Heights that she needed to sublet for six months. I took the blue line out to meet the friend of the friend, Eileen, and to see the sunshine palace, as Eileen calls it. I rented it right away. It costs $250 a month.

I'm talking to David Marks on the phone right now. He's this guy I have a crush on. I already have a boyfriend, Timmy

Waters. Both of them live in Northampton. On the weekends I've been taking the bus there, staying in my former apartment on North Street with Timmy Waters and sneaking around seeing David Marks, a guy with a Ph.D. and a high-paying job in the world of computers. He will turn out to be someone I would cross the street to get away from but I'm crazy about him in this moment and I believe that he can save me from all the misery I'm swimming around in now, the sense of being lost and lonely and just about every other bad feeling it's possible to have—I think that David Marks can rescue me from all that and I know Timmy Waters can't.

It's nighttime and the planes are booming overhead. The airport is close enough to smell the jet fuel when the planes are powering up, and all day long and most of the night I hear planes lumbering along the runway, roaring into the air, passing directly overhead, sometimes so loud they drown out whoever's on the other end of the phone. That keeps happening tonight as I talk to David Marks and I end our call and hang up.

Then I stand there looking through the bank of windows on the south side of the room. Out there I can see the Madonna Queen of the Universe sitting on top of Orient Avenue. The Queen of the Universe is a huge rectangular shrine with a 35-foot statue of the Madonna attached and a giant golden rectangular crown on top lit by spotlights below. Eileen told me when I came here to sublet the apartment from her that the Queen of the Universe is Boston's answer to the Statue of Liberty.

Behind me is a cluster of tables covered with flowerpots with all sorts of plants growing in them. There must be fifty plants here and every single one of them is dying. Two weeks ago I noticed little white blobs on some of them—mealy bugs, which I recognized because I've had them before. I tried washing them off with cotton swabs dipped in rubbing alcohol but the mealy bugs spread anyway, and now all of those plants are drooping in their pots. I'm glad I won't be here in a month when Eileen comes back from wherever she's gone and finds out that all the beloved plants in her sunshine palace have died. It doesn't matter that I did nothing to introduce those mealy bugs to those plants. I know it's all my fault they're dying and Eileen is going to be very upset with me when she finds out.

That's how I feel about Timmy Waters too, about the fact that I'm talking to some other guy while Timmy Waters is sitting around with no clue playing his guitar in the apartment we shared in Northampton, with my dog, surrounded by my stuff. I'm going to have to do something about that but not today. I go back to my chair and make another phone call.

Now it's the next day and I'm on the T, the blue line, going home from work at the end of the day. The train starts out below ground like all the other lines but at this point it's above ground, and I stare out the window as it careens along between stations. I see buildings and parking lots and wires and telephone poles. At one point we pass a car on fire in an empty lot. The train screeches to a halt at Wood Island stop; the doors open and a couple of people get off and the train starts up again.

I could not feel more lost than I am in this moment, traveling from one blue line station to another like a soul adrift in purgatory. I'm lost in time and space; lost in my twenties, some way station between childhood and the real adulthood of my thirties and forties; lost in East Boston, a part of the world that couldn't be more different from the rolling blue mountains and gentle college towns I come from in the other part of the state. And most of all I'm lost to myself. I'm a few steps farther away from love and happiness and home and family than I was before and I was already pretty far away then too and that's how I come to be in this purgatory, this place that feels to me like no place, no place at all.

My train arrives at Orient Heights, the fourth to the last stop on the blue line, and I get out and climb the steep hill to the house where my apartment is on the second floor. Along the way I pass many ordinary looking, even pretty, two- and three-story houses, houses where families live, people who are just like me. But it doesn't feel like they're like me.

This is not the Boston my mother lived in back in the late 1950s, not the Boston of the Fenway or Emerson College or 77 Gainsborough Street, a big rambling apartment building where about four years after my mother lived there the Boston Strangler strangled his first victim with a belt. My mother worked as a secretary at Emerson College when she lived in that building, having stayed in the city, officially separated from my father on the way to getting divorced although they never managed to do the latter, when she got out of a New Bedford psych ward. During the week my sister and I spent with her when I was three, I got locked in the bathroom in her apartment and was afraid of the swan boats and was terrified of my mother from beginning to end.

This part of Boston, East Boston, has a whole different feel than that did, the two different sections completely separate and alien from each other, as is true of so many parts of this city, and it doesn't occur to me, in this moment in 1978, that on some level I might be remembering that early trip, when I was three and my sister was five and we went to Boston on a Peter Pan bus with my father and were left behind to stay alone in an apartment with my mother for seven days. Maybe all that is still inside me, contributing to my feeling of being lost and sad and scared in this moment, but if it is I don't know it. It won't be another thirty or maybe forty years before that thought will occur to me.

I'm lying on my bed reading in my new apartment in Allston. I moved here with Margaret, my friend who's a secretary, like me, in the College Division at Little, Brown.  Margaret has straight brown hair and big teeth.  She's an artist of sorts and whenever she writes me a note or sends me a card, which is often, she draws a picture on it of a rabbit with big ears and huge rabbity teeth, like a sly comment on her own appearance. She says I'm her best friend and I tell her she's my best friend although the truth is I don't know her very well and I'm always holding something back in our friendship.  We decided to get an apartment together when my lease ran out at the sunshine palace.  Margaret wanted to move to Allston because she has a boyfriend here, he lives around the corner from this apartment.  She stays at his place every night and although she says she loves living with me I hardly ever see her, just once a day for a little while at dinnertime, and then sometimes at work.

So I'm here alone right now as I am every night.  There are cockroaches in this apartment, they come out at night when the lights are off.  If you go into the kitchen and turn on the light they scurry away and hide, displaying their creepy bug intelligence.  I hate living here because of them and for a bunch of other reasons:  the stink of cat pee in the vast tiled foyer, the view from the train as it chugs along Commonwealth Avenue on my way back forth to work:  car dealerships with little red and blue triangular flags strung up on ropes trying but failing to look cheerful, and shyster-y-looking insurance agencies and crisscrossing trolley wires and many rows of brick apartment buildings where B.U. students live.  The students are having fun in there, I'm sure of it, but even that makes my heart sink—the thought of those students in there having parties, smoking dope, studying just enough to get by only makes me feel even more like an alien.  There's nothing I like about this place.  It feels like one more step farther away from home and family and myself and even from the earth, warm and blue and familiar and safe.

I'm lying here on the fold-out couch reading a novel, *The French Lieutenant's Woman*, smelling the faint smell of bug killer that permeates the apartment. The room is full of boxes that I haven't unpacked and not much else. Margaret's over at her boyfriend's place like she always is. I look at the clock beside my bed. It's eleven, time to turn off the light and go to sleep, but first I have to go to the bathroom. I get up and tiptoe past the dark kitchen where the cockroaches live. I know that if I turn on the light I'll see them scurrying away across the stove, rushing to hide behind the refrigerator, moving along the wall on their way back down to the baseboards.

I've never seen one in the bathroom so it seems safe to go in there and besides what choice do I have. When I turn the bathroom light on tonight I don't see anything running away although I don't look very carefully; if there's a cockroach on the wall I'd rather not see it. I don't have my glasses on so everything is kind of blurry anyway. I sit down on the toilet and pee and turn to the toilet paper roll in the holder attached to the wall beside me. There's a little black spot on top of the roll and it occurs to me that it could be a cockroach but then I think, Oh surely not. I lean closer to get a better near-sighted look. And then I see it: *Yes! A cockroach!*

It's peeping over the toilet paper at me the way I'm peering over at it, and I jump up, turn off the light, and run from the room.

# Somerville

I'm sitting in the pink wingback chair by the window in my living room in Cambridge, reading *The Transit of Venus* by Shirley Hazzard, which I love.

This apartment is shaped like a train, all the rooms lined up in a row, one opening onto the next. My bedroom, a large room with many windows that looks out onto Wendell Street, is to the left of the front door. The front door opens into the living room—I can see the door from this chair—and then there's a small kitchen and beyond that is Patty's bedroom. There's a bathroom off the living room and outside the bathroom door, unrelated to what goes on in the bathroom, is a gray spot on the ceiling. It's damp and it's getting wetter, soggy even, but I don't know that. I just take that damp gray spot on the ceiling for granted, the way I take the other slightly shabby things about this apartment for granted.

It's about seven o'clock at night and I'm home alone; I'm still wearing my work clothes because I was too tired after my day at Little, Brown to even bother changing. The phone rings and I pick it up. It's my father. We make small talk for a few minutes and then he says hesitantly, his voice getting gravelly the way it does when he has to say something he doesn't want to say, "Your mother has cancer."

There's something uncertain and nervous in the way he says it, as if he's worried how I'll respond. I'm not sure whether he's afraid I'll be terribly upset and he doesn't want to upset me or what, but the effect of that note of hesitation is to make me downplay my own reaction even more than it's already downplayed by all the denial and history and separation from my mother that are heaped on top of it, smothering it into nothingness or almost.

I'm twenty-seven now and I've been in my mother's presence three times since I was eighteen. The first time I was crossing my sister's living room a little more than a year ago, looked out the window, and saw my father's truck pulling into the yard. I'd taken the Peter Pan bus from Boston to Northampton for the weekend as I often did and my father had picked me up at the station and driven me to my sister's house in Williamsburg, the town Christine and I went to junior high and high school in. Christine bought a rambling steel-blue Cape Cod house there in 1973 with the help of her daughter's father. My father occasionally made a sad face when he had to drive me to my sister's house instead of to his house where he and I could have a longer visit, the way he used to make a sad face when I wanted to stay at the Paysons' instead of going to his house as a kid. But unlike back then, his sadness didn't make me feel guilty, at least not very much, and besides, I had an excuse now: I was avoiding my mother. In my twenty-something-year-old, not-really-dealing-with-reality way, I thought I might never to have to be around her again.

And so it was a big shock to me, when I looked out the window as I was crossing my sister's living room, to see the ugly green truck my father was driving at the time pull up with not one but two people sitting in the cab. My father parked and got out the driver's side door, the passenger door opened and my mother stepped out onto my sister's lawn, and they both started walking toward the house. I briefly considered hiding in the closet or going into the bathroom and locking the door and pretending to myself and to everyone else that I wasn't here—making myself invisible, non-existent, like Alice shrinking down to nothing or almost nothing in *Through the Looking Glass*. But of course I knew I couldn't do that and so I stood rooted to the spot in the living room while my sister's front door opened and my mother followed my father into the house.

My mother said, stopping next to me in the middle of the floor, "If Mohammed won't go to the mountain, the mountain will come to Mohammed."

And then we all—my mother, father, sister, six-year-old niece, and I—sat down and had a normal visit together. At least as normal as a visit under the circumstances could be. Nobody said anything about how my mother and I hadn't seen each other in eight years, about the fact that I ran away from my parents' house and had never gone back or why, and all of that seemed to vanish in the same way I was hoping earlier that I would vanish, that is to say, not really, but sort of, because we pretended that it had.

I saw my mother again during a weekend visit to my sister's house in February and then again on Easter, and she didn't do or say anything to me that could be considered even remotely scary. But I couldn't stop being afraid of her. It was like all my childhood fear of her was still trapped somewhere inside me, not even under the surface in my unconscious but right there in my chest, in my throat, in my face, and I couldn't get it to go away.

"What kind of cancer does she have?" I say to my father now.

He tells me it's ovarian cancer, and then he tells me about a four-months-to-live prognosis and I say oh or something like it and then we go on to some other topic of conversation.

I don't go home to visit my mother right away, the way years later I will wish that I did and also wish I could say that I did. At the time I tell myself I'm too busy to go home, but the truth is that I can't deal with the drama, the heaviness of my mother's illness, with the fear of being exposed to my mother's emotions and the fear of my own emotions, which are hidden from me and which I want to keep hidden from myself. So I don't go. My mother has chemotherapy and radiation, loses her hair, gets sicker and sicker. Finally she's in the hospital and it's clear that she isn't going to come back out. My father informs me of that too, also on the phone, and says that I should take the bus to Northampton very soon if I want to see my mother before she dies.

My sister picks me up at the bus station in Northampton and drives me directly to the hospital to visit my mother. It's about one o'clock on a weekday afternoon. I've taken a couple of days off work. Christine parks in the hospital parking lot and we get out. As we walk across the pavement toward the building I'm so frightened I can barely breathe. My terror's a complicated mixture of my childhood fear of my mother and my own fear of disease, which is also, in some unconscious way it will be years before I can untangle, my fear of my mother, as if my mother has gotten transformed in my mind into *cancer* or some other fatal illness that can turn me into a helpless victim and then kill me.

Christine leads me to the elevator inside the hospital and pushes the up button. The elevator arrives and its silver doors open and my sister and I get in and Christine pushes the round 'four' button. The elevator stops at the fourth floor and I trail my sister down the hall past some empty wheelchairs and the nursing station and other patients' open doorways. Finally she turns into one of the rooms and through the doorway I see my mother lying on the bed with her eyes closed, her face gaunt and her stomach swollen and her arms emaciated and covered with bruises, an IV needle attached to a tube and taped to one of her wrists, a blond wig slightly askew on her head. I take a breath and follow my sister into the room.

"Hello!" Christine says in a hearty voice and my mother opens her eyes, looks at us, and blinks. Christine and I sit in chairs on either side of her.

"How are you?" I say awkwardly, trying to make my face take on a look that's both sympathetic and cheerful and that hides everything I'm really feeling:  that sickening terror of being here, which is a little better now that we're actually here but is still sitting in the pit of my stomach.

My mother raises her unencumbered arm and gestures toward the other parts of the room as if to say I can see for myself how she is and there's no point in trying to describe it and I nod earnestly and sympathetically to let her know I agree.

There are a few dishes with the barely touched remnants of my mother's hospital lunch resting on the bedside table—cottage cheese, red jello with fruit in it, something that looks like canned string beans—along with a plastic glass with a bent straw poking out of it. "I can't eat much anymore," my mother whispers. "Tell me what you've been eating."

I smile and recite a few things I've eaten today and then look at my sister hoping she'll take over the conversation. Just then a nurse's assistant bustles into the room and says cheerfully to my mother, "You've got some mail!"  The nurse's aid places a square envelope on the table and takes away the tray with my mother's food. I glance at the envelope, recognize the handwriting on it, and cringe.

My mother picks up the card, slowly opens it, and reads what it says. I can see from where I'm sitting that it's a Hallmark card with a lovely picture of violets on the front and a greeting of some sort printed in flowery script inside, the words, "Sincerely, Evelyn Payson" penned in neat, former-school-teacher handwriting at the bottom of the greeting.

I raise my eyes and stare across the room, bracing for my mother's reaction. Here it is, my mother and Mrs. Payson, the woman whose house I grew up in, crossing paths, the thing I feared and dreaded as a kid, because my mother hated Mrs. Payson so much we had to pretend she didn't exist. I briefly resent Mrs. Payson. *Don't you understand that you don't exist when we're around my mother,* I think, silently addressing her. *That the mere mention of your name sends her into one of her ranting fits?* And then I realize that of course Mrs. Payson doesn't understand that—she refuses to understand it in her good-hearted Christian way, and in her stubborn goodness she's sent my mother this stupid card and by some awful coincidence I have to be here when it arrives.

My mother places the card on the hospital tray. She's silent for a moment and then she says, staring across the room, not looking at me and Christine, "Your father always liked the Paysons because they gave him approval."

There's nothing my sister and I can say to that and we both sit there mutely.

My mother is tired and in pain. She flinches visibly several times, and after about fifteen minutes my sister and I stand up to leave. My sister bends over and kisses my mother on the cheek. I just stand there by the bed, not knowing what to do. I've never kissed my mother and she's never kissed me and I can't imagine bending down to her emaciated face now and touching my lips to her forehead or cheek.

My mother seems to understand. She holds her hand out to me and I take it for a moment. Then she releases her grasp, closes her eyes, and turns her face away, and my sister and I tiptoe from the room.

Now Christine and I are in a diner in Northampton, standing by the cash register waiting to pay for our lunch. I'm going to take the bus back to Boston instead of staying overnight, then come back here on the weekend to visit my mother for what will surely be the last time. I can't wait to get away, can already feel some of the relief I'll experience as I board the bus and sit in a window seat in its air-conditioned interior and am driven back to Boston and the lonely, neutral anonymity of my life there. But suddenly the piped-in music from a local radio station is interrupted by an urgent announcement: A tanker truck carrying a toxic chemical has been hit by a train in a railroad switching yard in Somerville. I hear "Monsanto," "trichloride," "toxic fog drifting over parts of Cambridge," "evacuation."

"Oh my God," I say to Christine. "Did you hear that?"

"What?"

"Shh. It's coming on again."

Christine and I stand beside the cash register, change in hand, listening tensely while the radio announcer says again, his voice full of urgency and importance, that a tank truck has been hit in Somerville spilling toxic chemicals and that a cloud of poisonous gas has formed. They don't know yet where and how far the gas is expected to spread. For now only people in Somerville and certain parts of Cambridge are being evacuated, but listeners should stay tuned to find out when and if people from any other parts of the Boston region should leave. In the meantime, everyone not in the immediate area being evacuated should keep their windows closed and stay in their homes if at all possible.

"I can't believe this," I say to my sister. Panic spreads through me like floodwater rising in a basement. At this time in my life I'm filled with fear about everything but so far I haven't been exposed to any of the real things in the world that most people are afraid of; everything I know about disasters I know through the fear-mongering TV news and the small-town, country-people reactions of the Paysons and my father. So things that might seem relatively minor, only mildly threatening, to people who live in cities and deal with problems every day seem enormous to me and will continue to affect me that way for a long time.   And now, when I hear about the toxic chemical spill in this moment when my mother is in the hospital dying and I'm dying to get away from her, my reaction is out of proportion.   Not only because the words toxic chemical and poisonous gas conjure up images in my mind almost as terrifying as nuclear war would be to some people, but also because the chemical spill, this horrible nightmare in the world, means that now I'm trapped in the private nightmare of my mother dying in the hospital and all that means to me.

"I can't go back to Cambridge," I say to Christine.   She looks at me wide-eyed and we leave the restaurant and begin walking down the sidewalk, past the bus station, to her car parked in the Greyhound station parking lot.

When we get to her house in Williamsburg I call my office at the publishing company, where they're expecting me back at work the next day, and tell them I'll be staying away indefinitely due to the chemical spill.   I expect my boss to strongly agree with my decision and urge me to stay away—in fact I'm surprised that he's still there in his office, answering the phone so nonchalantly, considering the disaster that's going on.   But he seems somewhat taken aback that I'll be missing even more work, surprised that I'm taking the spill in Somerville, so far from our office, so seriously.

"Well, all right," he says. "But we hope to see you soon."

That night when my father calls my sister, she tells him about the problem in the Boston area and says that I'll be staying for a few extra days.   The next day Christine and I hang around her house talking and cooking and eating and doing the sorts of other non-productive things you do when someone is visiting.   Neither of us says anything about my mother or about going to see her in the hospital again.   That night my father comes by at about six o'clock in the evening. He says that he visited my mother on his way home from work and that she wants all three of us—him, my sister, and me—to go to the hospital at an appointed time the following day to talk about what happened in our family.

"She wants us all to *talk*," my father says. He looks nervous, skeptical, and displeased. "She has something she wants to say about when you girls were small. There's a social worker who's going to sit with us too. This whole thing was probably all the social worker's idea."

"Not necessarily," says my sister. "I think it's a good idea."

"What about you, Mary?" my father says. "Are you willing to do that?"

"Sure," I say, trying to strike the right balance between what I think my father wants me to feel and say and what I think the right thing to do is and what I really feel. More than anything I'm surprised and sort of impressed by my mother's request. To my knowledge she has never shown any interest in talking, really getting honest about things, before. I'm the one in the family who has always been most interested in talking and writing about feelings and about what happened in the past to try to come to terms with it. I'm not going to a therapist at this time but I'll start going to one in a few years. My sister isn't quite as motivated in her life as I am by the drive and quest for healing, but she's excited and enthusiastic about my mother's request to try to sort some things out with a professional on hand, on this April day in 1980. I find that I am too, once my father leaves to go home.

"I think it's going to be great!" Christine says.

"Me too," I agree.

The next day, in my mother's hospital room, the social worker, a pudgy, mild-mannered man, looks at us expectantly through wire-rimmed glasses and smiles. He's sitting in a chair beside my mother's bed, holding a pen poised over a pad of paper. I can see that he's a nice man and that we have nothing to fear from him and I relax. My father, my sister, and I are sitting in chairs situated haphazardly around the room: my sister's chair is at the bottom of my mother's bed, I'm beside the social worker, and my father's in a chair opposite me on other side of my mother.

"I wanted us to talk about some things that happened, and I thought it might be helpful if there was someone here with us, so I asked Ed to join us," my mother begins, gesturing toward the bespectacled social worker.

Ed smiles and looks around the room at each of us, making eye contact in a friendly acknowledging way.

"Great!" Christine says and I nod. My father shifts awkwardly in his chair.

"I was in and out of the hospital when you girls were little," my mother says. "I left you at home with your father. When I came back you were hungry and your diapers were wet because your father had neglected you and you were crying because you wanted your mommy and ..."

I stop listening. Ed continues to look at my mother in a friendly interested way, taking occasional notes on his pad of paper, but I sit in my chair staring down at the floor. I expected my mother to say something that would shed light on our family history—explain why she never divorced my father after getting so close to it, or describe how she was overtaken by mental illness after I was born and why she couldn't bond with me and what effect that had on her, or tell us something else startling that we didn't know before. But the picture she's painting of Christine and me as babies crying for our mommy is so far off what I know to be true I give up on learning anything new.

My father makes some weak attempts to defend himself

by contradicting my mother and they argue back and forth a little. I feel sorry for them both; obscurely embarrassed that even now, so close to the end of her life, my mother's still blaming my father for all our problems; sad for her that she's still fixated on that old battle with him. And disappointment rises up in me like water surging over a dam. There isn't going to be an answer. We aren't going to delve into the truth with the help of a social worker today.

I take the bus back to Boston the next day. The following Friday I return to Western Massachusetts. My father picks me up at the station in Northampton and brings me to my sister's, saying that he'll come in the morning to take me to visit my mother one last time. He also says that he stopped by the hospital to see her that evening and she was in very bad shape. "I just sat beside the bed and held her hand," he says. "She was all curled up in a fetal position like a baby."

When he calls in the morning at eight a.m. to say that my mother died in the night, I feel sort of like a kid finding out that school has been cancelled because of a snowstorm. And then I feel guilty about feeling like that. I know I should be sorry I didn't have a chance to see her one last time, but I also know I couldn't have faced seeing her, the terrifying specter of my childhood, curled up in a fetal position with nothing between her and death except the last tattered remnants of her physical self.

My father says that he can come over and pick me up and take me to his house, and since I'm alone at Christine's—she and her daughter both just left, Christine for work, Leonika for school—and since I'm so relieved not to be going to the hospital to see my mother, I'm happy to agree. My father shows up and we drive to his house and go inside and sit at the kitchen table.

"I saw your mother last night at about six o'clock in the hospital," he says, repeating what he told me in the car the previous evening. "I sat beside her and held her hand. She was curled up on the bed in fetal position. I don't think she even knew I was there."

He gives me a nervous, slightly tentative look, as if there's something a little painful to him in the situation, though I can't tell what. Then it comes to me that his anxiety has to do with how I'm going to react. And then I have the sudden awful realization that he's nervous that I might be sad about my mother's death. That he's afraid that if I am sad, my sorrow might make me love her more and therefore love him less. That it has always been this way between the three of us, me reassuring my father, my father and I reassuring ourselves at my mother's expense, my father making sure he got all the love and my mother got none. All of that comes to me in a split second as I'm sitting there at the kitchen table, and then I suppress it because it's too painful and embarrassing to see, to know that about my father and myself.

But way down deep inside myself, past the desire not to deal with who my father has become and who my mother was and the ugliness of their relationship and my part in it all, past all that, buried beneath it like some small bodily organ hidden under a bunch of other organs and layers of fat and ganglia and viscera and other un-nameable blood and guts, is a deep feeling of misery and shame, of alienation from my father and therefore from myself, that will stay with me for years after that, until not long before my father dies himself.

The phone rings and he gets up and walks slowly across the kitchen to answer it. He picks up the receiver and holds it to his ear. "Hello?" he says tentatively, as if he can't imagine who could possibly be calling. The thought flashes through my mind that whoever it is, is calling to inform him of my mother's death, as if we've hit an empty pocket of time and been thrown backwards by nine or ten hours.

"Yes," my father says. "This is the home of Lois. No, no, I'm afraid she's not here. She died last night.

"No, no, I don't think I have any need for that," he says after a pause while he listens to whoever's talking to him on the other end. "All right then," he says. "Thank you for calling." He carefully replaces the receiver and returns to the kitchen table.

"That was somebody from Goodwill," he says. "Your mother ordered some special expensive light bulbs from them months ago and now they want to deliver them. Part of the money goes to poor people, but I don't think I should pay $2.50 for a light bulb, do you?"

"No," I say, "I wouldn't." And after that we sit there at the kitchen table, not looking at each other, not saying anything, for what seems like hours. The fan in the refrigerator hums, a board creaks somewhere in the other room, I hear my father breathing.

The next day I take the bus to Boston, take the red line to Harvard Square, walk home to my apartment on Wendell Street. I unlock the door and go inside and then I see it: a gray pile of something on the floor outside the bathroom. Wet plaster. The ceiling has collapsed and there's a ragged opening, not to the sky but to the beams and wires above the ceiling. I call my landlord's number and his girlfriend, Dorothy, tells me he's out of town. She's full of alarm and sympathy. She says she'll call him right away and if she can't get hold of him she'll find someone to fix the ceiling anyway. I tell her my mother just died and she's full of even more sympathy. She's sad for me and worried and concerned on my behalf, imagining my sorrow and on top of that me having to deal with this apartment disaster.

But I'm not worried. I'm not even sad, although I can't tell her that. I wonder what she would do or think or say if I did tell her that. But I know I can't. For one thing, I don't know what I would say; I don't even know exactly what's going on inside myself. I just know that there's a flat gray spot inside me where the feelings should be, like the flat gray newly plastered place on the ceiling the next day, after the guy Dorothy hired has come and fixed it.

# Blue Blotter

I'm perching on a plastic chair in a gray-carpeted waiting area in Logan Airport, staring through a wall-size glass window. It's nighttime and outside, parked on the tarmac, inching along runways, roaring down takeoff strips and lumbering into the air, are airplanes.

My classmates and I are here on a field trip to the airport, getting desensitized. We were driven here in a van by Mr. Smith, whom we've each paid $350 to get over our fear of flying. We've been attending classes for a month now, learning how diet contributes to anxiety and practicing relaxation exercises, and next week we're going to be going up in an actual airplane.

I'm taking this class because I have a phobia of flying and a phobia of public speaking and I have to fly to New York in two weeks and give a sales presentation. I scraped and clawed my way up the ladder at Little, Brown, right up to the point where I was going to have to start flying places and giving public speeches, and then I quit and took a job as an editor at an obscure little publishing business in a different part of Boston. I thought I was taking a good job in a growing company, but it turned out I was basically signing up to be a glorified secretary in a large print division. After six months I transferred to another department and talked the president and the vice president of the company into letting me find some out-of-print books that could be reprinted in trade paperback editions. I went to the Cambridge Public Library and picked six old books that I thought people might still be interested in. I called their original publishers and acquired rights to them, and the company set about the business of publishing them—designers designing covers and production people getting bids from printers and a whole lot of other rigmarole. A sales force has been hired and on a certain date I'm going to have to fly to New York and give a little speech to them so they can go out and sell the books to bookstores. So far in my life I've managed to avoid flying and public speaking and to more or less hide my phobias from myself and everybody else, but I've known all along I was going to have to fly somewhere and talk in front of people eventually, and now here it is.

To deal with my phobia of public speaking I've taken a four-week class at the Public Speaking Institute, where they told us how to prepare by making an outline and how to relax before we gave our speech by breathing deeply and some other things. On the last week of the class everyone had to get up and give a little talk. I was so nervous during my speech I could hardly get any words out and even the teacher seemed embarrassed for me. At the end of my talk she said I probably wasn't ready to give an actual speech in public, although I had told her before that I did have to give a talk at the end of the month. I sat back down feeling like I belonged to some other species than the species the rest of the class belonged to, feeling hopeless about my ability to function in the world the way other people did and the way I knew I was going to have to.

It's as if something has me by the throat and will not let me go. It's the cumulative effects of my entire childhood, of course it is. It's my mother looming over me on the inner stage of my consciousness, all that heart-stopping lion-rushing-toward-you terror of her, all that trying to make myself invisible. But I haven't even begun to scratch the surface of all the old impacted pain inside myself, and I don't know that's what has me by the throat. I just know it's more powerful than I am and certainly more powerful than any deep breathing exercises and hints and tips about how to prepare and organize a speech. I know it's so powerful nothing will make it go away, but I'm still hoping that something will make it go away. For the time being, though, I've given up on the public speaking component of my problem and moved on to the flying part of my problem.

To try to solve that I took this fear of flying class with Mr. Smith. Mr. Smith believes that the cause of most nervousness is food allergies, and he made us hold various bits of food in our hands, corn kernels, wheat berries, peanuts, soybeans, and then he came along and pushed down on our arms; if your arm goes down easily that means you're allergic to the thing you're holding. The idea is that if you don't eat whatever you're allergic to before your flight you'll be calm. He also told us not to eat sugar doughnuts before our flights because everyone's allergic to sugar, and he taught us how to relax various parts of our bodies, toes, ankles, calves, buttocks, et cetera, by clenching and then relaxing them. We're supposed to practice our relaxation exercises at home and when we come into class he walks us through them. He's a short heavy man with a restless, impatient manner and there's something slightly imperious in the way he tells us in class every week, "Now tense your buttocks, now hold … hold … hold, now release." He has an assistant, a young woman, who walks around among us while he tells us what to do, and sometimes she presses down on our arms or shoulders to help us relax.

It turns out I'm allergic to corn kernels and wheat berries, but finding this out will do nothing whatsoever to alleviate my fear of flying because no sugar doughnut or corn kernel or any other food item or its absence is going to cure my fear of flying, and neither is any relaxation exercise, although I do the relaxation exercises to the best of my ability. Sometimes Mr. Smith gets irritable and yells at us because we haven't been practicing our relaxation exercises enough at home. So in addition to being terrified of flying and knowing that at the end of the class I'm going to have to go up in an airplane, not to mention knowing that in a few weeks I'm going to have to fly to New York and give a sales presentation, now I'm nervous because there's an angry man who's angry because I'm not adequately relaxing during the relaxation exercises.

I've started having panic attacks during the relaxation exercises. As soon as we close our eyes and slow our breathing and start clenching and unclenching our whatevers, an enormous white-hot anxiety rises up in me and I feel like I'm going to die.

So the next day after the night when we watch the airplanes at the airport, I decide to quit the fear of flying workshop. I'm going to lose all the money I paid to take it, but I don't care.

I know perfectly well, of course, that it's safe to fly on airplanes and get up and talk in front of others, that other people do these things easily, safely, confidently, all the time. I know that, and yet I can't dislodge the irrational feeling that somehow *I* can't fly on an airplane, *I* can't talk to a group of people, and if I try something terrible will happen: My plane will crash or explode on the runway, I'll stand up in front of those people and . . . I can't even imagine what will happen when I try to do that.

And yet, I'm going to have to do it: The date is set for my little speech, the plane reservations have been made by my company, the tickets are in the hands of the company travel agent, everyone in the company knows I'm going to do it, I know I'm going to do it. And yet I also know that I can't do it.

Finally, at the last minute, someone refers me to a hypnotherapist who has an office in Cambridge City Hospital near Central Square.

Charlie Ducey tells me to close my eyes and visualize myself going down a set of stairs. I do and on a landing I see, in my mind's eye, old dented paint cans.

"Very evocative," Charlie Ducey says in his kind soothing voice.

He tells me that at the bottom of the stairs I'm going to see a stage and when the curtains open there's going to be something on the stage that will tell me something about my fear of public speaking. I see the stage in the Westhampton town hall, which had blond wooden floors and smelled like chalk dust. The curtain opens bit by bit and there on the stage is my mother yelling at me.

This isn't exactly surprising to me. I've known all along on some level that my public speaking phobia has to do with the fact that I'm projecting my mother onto the audience—and I don't feel especially confident that seeing her on a stage in a trance will make a whole lot of difference, although Charlie Ducey seems to think it will and that now I'll be able to give my little speech with no problem. While I'm still in my trance, he "suggests" that I won't be frightened on the plane and if I am I'll think of him and then I'll stop being afraid. And that's that.

I leave his office feeling apprehensive that what he did won't work, but it must have worked, because the next week I fly to New York and give my little speech and it's no big deal at all. Sitting on the plane going home I think, *Is this really what I was so afraid of?* And I know that it isn't. I know that all that fear was an internal event, that it had almost nothing to do with anything in the outside everyday world.

The really significant thing I ended up getting from going to Charlie Ducey to be hypnotized to get over my fear of flying and my fear of public speaking was hypnosis itself. I loved hypnosis—loved that feeling of sitting in an office going to another place inside myself—and a few days after my sales presentation I went back to Charlie Ducey and said, "I want you to be my therapist, I want to keep coming to you and have you hypnotize me some more." So that's what we did.


It's early Wednesday morning and I'm sitting on the leather couch in Charlie Ducey's office and Charlie Ducey says, "So, shall we do a little hypnosis?"

I've been doing this for a couple of months now, coming to this office once a week before work. Afterwards I take the subway from Central Square to Park Street and walk from there to the little publishing company.

I nod and settle myself on the couch and then he says, in his kind, mild-mannered, non-threatening voice, "Close your eyes and picture yourself in an elevator." The imaginary elevator has numbers above its doors and as it descends the numbers descend, the elevator and the numbers go down, down, down, 10, 9, 8, 7, 6, 5, 4. When the elevator arrives at the bottom floor the doors open and I get out and see where I am. Sometimes instead of riding the elevator I just go down a set of stairs, like I did during my first session when I saw the paint cans on the landing. It's those paint cans that I love, them and every other thing I see in these trances, along with the feeling of being hypnotized itself, a kind of prickly, buoyant feeling, as if you're entering some atmosphere that's slightly thicker, more gelatinous than air.

Today in my trance I find myself sitting in one of those wooden school chairs with the arm that wraps around to make a little desktop. There's a pen in my hand and the tip is poised on a pad of paper.

"Why don't you write something?" Charlie Ducey asks.

"No!" I say in a babyish way. Sometimes in my trances I suddenly go from feeling like an adult to feeling like a child, as if my inner child, that poor neglected mashed-down child version of myself, is inside me there—wherever *there* is, that alternate interior universe that I go down down down to, like Alice going down the rabbit hole—just waiting to step forward so I can put her on or she can put on me like a set of clothing.

"I don't understand," Charlie Ducey says. "Why don't you want to write something on the paper?"

"Because then you'll know the thoughts that are in my head!" I say in a loud, childish voice.

"Okay," says Charlie Ducey. He pauses, then asks, "Is there anything else you notice where you are?"

I say that the spot where I'm sitting has transformed from a wrap-around chair into a regular school desk and there's a blotter on the desktop. Charlie Ducey asks me what color the blotter is and I say it's a nasty spongy-looking pea green.

"Why don't you get rid of it and replace it with one that's a different color?" Charlie Ducey says.

"I'll try," I say dubiously, and all of a sudden the blotter goes from ugly pea green to an indescribably beautiful blue, a pale, airy, celestial blue, the most beautiful blue in the universe.

"Amazing," Charlie Ducey says.

The next time I go to him I get on a cloud and the cloud takes me somewhere:  to Stanley Park in Vancouver. In real life I spent a couple of months in Vancouver in 1977 with Timmy Waters, the boyfriend I dumped for David Marks after I moved to Boston, and now I'm in Stanley Park in the Vancouver of my memories transformed into the Vancouver of my trance. There's a green metal box sitting on the ground; the box is locked and there's a little key lying in the dirt beside it. It's a shallow, rectangular, slightly beat-up metal box. It looks vaguely familiar but I won't figure out why for almost twenty-five years. What I do know right now is what's in it: *toys*, the most fun, exciting toys in the universe, toys that radiate the feeling you get when you play for hours on end without thought of yourself or anything else.

"Why don't you pick up the key and open the box?" Charlie Ducey says in his kind soothing voice.

"I can't!"

"Why not?" Charlie Ducey asks.

"Because those toys can't be mine," I say, my voice rising to a pitiful wail with an undercurrent of irritation, as if Charlie Ducey's making me state a painful but obvious fact.

"Oh," Charlie Ducey says.

Our hour was almost over and we didn't have time to discuss what those toys were all about, but it seems fairly obvious in retrospect that they were symbols for creativity, and that the same inner whatever that was stopping me from talking in public and keeping me on the ground—holding me back, really, from moving forward in my life—was making me feel like I had no right to own my own psychic toys inside my own box. Still, just knowing they were locked away like that must've solved some problem on some level, because the next week when I see Charlie Ducey I say, "I've decided I want to be a writer."

My new roommate Patty is a writer. We live together in a rent-controlled apartment in Cambridge, which I got by calling my friend Ron's old landlord and asking him if he had anything available in Cambridge and, as unlikely as it seems, he did. It feels lighter, airier, happier, freer here to me, and even though my path will continue to take me through many dark places and I'll encounter many obstacles, if I had to choose a moment in my life when things started to get better instead of worse, when I turned around and started heading away from the darkness toward the light, it might be when I got to move from Allston to Wendell Street in Cambridge.  Or it might be this moment in Charley Ducey's office.

Patty has an MFA and spends her spare time sitting at the kitchen table working on short stories, and sometimes she says, "Mary! I'm pulling my hair out with this revision!" Patty's living the writer's life; she goes to writing colonies and finishes stories no matter how hard it is and sends her short stories to contests; she won the Nelson Algren award for a short story and pretty soon she will get a Stegner fellowship at Stanford and move away.

I've always wanted to be a writer, and when I got out of college I took a clerical job and tried to write, but what I was writing wasn't any good and I gave up on being a writer, took that job at Little, Brown, and moved to Boston.  Something has been dawning on me for a while, although it hasn't completely risen to the surface of my consciousness until right now in Charlie Ducey's office:  I want what Patty has.  I want to sit at the kitchen table and pull my hair out over a revision. I even envy her problems, the rejection and the fear of rejection and the writing never being good enough.

It's seven o'clock in the morning when the words "I want to be a writer" pop out of my half-asleep mouth in Charlie Ducey's office. I didn't know I was going to say them. But now that I have, I know they're true.

A month later I will quit my job at the obscure little publishing company, the last full-time job I've ever had, become a freelance editor, and start writing. I'm going to be a writer, I'll say to anyone who will listen, and nothing short of death is going to stop me.   Many people will try to talk me out of it. My old boss at Little, Brown will say, in a hope-belittling way, "So, you're going to write the great American novel," and my last boss, the vice president of the small publishing company, will assure me when I quit that I will be miserable not working at a company, and everyone, including Charlie Ducey one minute from now, will point out that there's not much money in being a writer and I'm signing on to a life of poverty and insecurity. But I won't care. I will feel like I've been lost but now I'm found, and what I've found is myself.

I'll write some short stories and apply to the Iowa Writers' Workshop. I'll leave Boston and move to Iowa City, and it will be many years before I find some other way to get down the stairs into that vast airy mysterious inner world that I had my first encounter with in Charlie Ducey's office.

# The Nightmare Years

I'm seated in a wine-colored wingback chair in a large living room in Lenox, Massachusetts. There are stacks of books on the coffee table and the floor, a faded oriental rug, a fireplace to my right, a bank of windows about ten feet away on the left. Across from me, sitting in his own armchair, looking at me over the tops of his glasses, is a famous old man, a writer.

He's eighty-two years old and I'm twenty-six years old. I'm still working at Little, Brown, as an editorial assistant in the trade division, at this moment, and I've driven here to help him pick the photos for his newly finished, about-to-be-published-by-Little, Brown memoir, *The Nightmare Years, 1930-1940*, which is partly about his years living in Germany during the reign of Hitler and the Nazis. I've done some editing on the manuscript for that book, crossing out small superfluous chunks of language from many paragraphs and sentences, because the manuscript he handed in was way too long and his editor didn't have time to cut it.

I've driven to his house to help pick out the photos for the book. The editor's here now too, but he's in the bathroom at this moment. He came from New York and I came from Boston; his rental car was in the driveway when I arrived in my rental car. There was a slip of paper taped to the front door that said, in spidery and somehow literary-looking old-man handwriting, "Knock loud and come in." I knocked loud and went in, tiptoed through a big old-fashioned kitchen to the dining room where I found the writer and the editor seated at a long dining room table going through a pile of photos.

"Let's ask Mary Allen what she thinks," the writer, William L. Shirer, author of *The Rise and Fall of the Third Reich* and many other books, said in a jovial way, handing me a 5 by 7 glossy print. It showed a row of corpses dangling by the neck from ropes slung over a wooden scaffold in a field, a handful of soldiers looking on—something about an uprising in Afghanistan in the 1920s where he had his first assignment as a reporter, I would learn in a few minutes. "Do you think that picture's too grim to be in the book?" William Shirer asked me. I said I didn't think so and he turned triumphantly to the editor and said, "See? Mary Allen doesn't mind it."

He's short and mostly bald and has a glass eye—later I'll learn he lost the real one on the ski slopes of Austria when he fell and poked it out with a ski pole, skiing with his first wife before the war. He's not at all my type, even if he was forty or fifty years younger, but the aura of history that surrounds him, not to mention his stature as one of the most successful writers of the twentieth century, give him an allure that's hard to ignore.

I'm terrified of him in this moment as we sit in the living room, his editor, Roger Donald, having conveniently disappeared into the bathroom; I can't wait to get away from Bill, as he insists I call him. But nevertheless I feel compelled to seize the moment to tell him what he will find out anyway the next time he calls Little, Brown and asks for me: I've only got a week left in my job and then I'm going to start working somewhere else. So I tell him that, and somehow I have the nerve to tell him that although I'm working in publishing right now I think I might want to be a writer, and he looks at me closely over his glasses and says, "Don't wait too long." He tells me that a writer writes and that I should pick a certain amount of time, maybe two hours, to fit writing into my life five days a week. And then he says, "Maybe we can have dinner the next time I come to Boston." He hands me a piece of paper and tells me to write down my phone number and I do, thinking that of course I will never see him again.

So I'm shocked when my phone rings on a Sunday night two weeks later and it's him. He tells me he has to be in Boston this week and would I like to have dinner with him on Thursday. I'm so nervous I can hardly breathe but I say in a normal cheerful voice—I was good at faking it back then—that I would love to have dinner with him, and he suggests we meet in Locke-Ober, a fancy restaurant my boss at Little, Brown used to take authors to for lunch before he was fired six months ago. The very idea that I am going to Locke-Ober to meet William Shirer for dinner is so alarming and preposterous I can barely think about it, but on Thursday evening I take the subway to Park Street, cross Tremont Street, and find Locke-Ober on Winter Street. Bill is there waiting for me and we have dinner, talking about this and that in a friendly getting-to-know-you sort of way, him looking at me over his glasses as if I am fascinating, me smiling, acting interested, faking it the whole time. Two weeks after that he calls me and invites me up to his house for the weekend. I can take the bus on Friday and come back on Sunday. I don't know how to say no so I say yes, I would love to do that.

I'm going to be staying in a little guest room upstairs, I find out when I get there. There's a single bed in the guest room and a gray metal four-drawer filing cabinet. On top of the cabinet is a copy of a letter typed with an old-fashioned typewriter—he still uses that typewriter, a big black Olivetti, for all his writing, I will find out the next day when he shows me his study. The letter on top of the filing cabinet is dated March 30, 1952. It's Bill protesting something that was done to him related to the loyalty oaths and Joseph McCarthy; I don't exactly understand what as I stand there reading the letter. I will never quite understand no matter how many times I read that letter, which will be sitting on top of the filing cabinet, apparently waiting to be filed, every time I come here.

The next day we drive around town in his modest blue Chevy running errands, going to the grocery store, the library, the copy store. "Are you an author?" the young girl working behind the counter at the copy store asks him shyly. He tells her yes, and the girl says she learned about his book in school. Afterwards as we're getting into the car he grins at me slyly and jokes, "I arranged that to impress you." In the evening we make dinner together in his big old-fashioned kitchen. We decide to roast a chicken but neither of us has ever done that before and we don't know which side to put facing up. In the end we do it wrong, with the breast side down, and it takes so long for the chicken to cook we have to give up and eat something else. He will tell that story over and over, laughing affectionately, as if it gives him pleasure that neither of us knows how to cook a chicken.

His interest in me, his unwavering flattering attention that first weekend and on many other weekends to come, makes me feel special, although I don't quite know what to make of it or what to do with it. I have stumbled into his purview like a gnat wandering into a spider web and he has woven the threads of his awareness around me. He doesn't want to capture me and eat me, he wants to *see* me, to examine me from this angle and that, as he has done with everyone and everything he's encountered throughout his adult life. He's encountered important people, witnessed historic events: Gandhi, whom he interviewed, following him around for days talking to him when he, Bill, was a cub reporter for the Chicago Tribune—he wrote a book about that. He tells me Gandhi always had time for everything and that's the mark of a great man; he himself never has enough time for anything, he adds offhandedly. Hemingway, or Hemmy as he sometimes calls him; in his day everyone was writing novels copying Hemingway, even he wrote a novel copying Hemingway. The Joyces, he saw them having dinner in a restaurant once in Paris with their daughter Lucia who was schizophrenic; F. Scott Fitzgerald and Tom Eliot, as he calls him, and other writers he knew in the Paris of the twenties. Isadora Duncan; he had a big crush on her but she said he was too young for her. Most of all, later, in Berlin, Hitler and the other Nazis, Goering, Hess, plus the huge rallies he attended and is still haunted by in nightmares. All of that he's seen in his day and more, he has observed it, noted it down on his reporter's notepad, paid copious attention to it. And now he's paying attention to me.

He asks me what I think about this and that and listens fully to my answers as if they really matter; he looks at me closely over the tops of his glasses. All this looking and listening to, all this being seen, is kind of nice. I am in the company of Gandhi and Hemingway and T.S. Eliot—I know things about them no one else knows, how Gandhi said he *had* to sleep with those girls to keep him warm but it wasn't really about that; which Nazis were truly vicious assholes and which ones weren't too bad; how X, a big-time writer, had an unhappy marriage and brought up paper bags full of booze when he came to visit. He tells me these things as if I'm part of the crowd, just another famous person or a future famous person. He is convinced that I will be a somebody in the world. Once he says to me, after telling me how he had to make money by being on the speaker circuit after he lost his job and his income potential during the McCarthy hearings, *I wonder what kind of public speaker you'll be.* I nod and smile when he says this, warming to his vision of me as a future great person. I don't tell him that I have a phobia of public speaking and had to quit my job at Little, Brown because it was getting to the point where I might have to speak at a sales conference. I am still hiding, transforming, trapped in a cocoon woven out of my own fear in this part of my life, but of course I don't tell him that. I barely know it myself and when I'm in his presence I let myself forget it. When I'm with him part of me starts to believe I can be a great person or at least gets used to thinking of him thinking of me that way.

But when he tries to take my picture it throws me into a panic. I am not photogenic: I can't stand to look at pictures of myself. In the most hidden part of myself I'm trying to be invisible; I can't see myself and I have an absolute terror of being seen. I have to hide the thing in me that I think is ugly, from myself as well as everyone else; it's something buried deep inside me, although maybe not buried as deeply as I think it is. This is why I can't have my picture taken, why I can't speak in front of others—because if I do, that thing inside me will show itself and others will see it. It will take me another thirty years or so to come to understand what that's all about, even more time to dispel it, to dig up that deep hidden ugliness and expose it to the light and air where it can disappear like a monster in a child's video game. Although of course it's not a monster but a suppressed tornado of sadness and shame planted inside me by my mother, perhaps even partly belonging to my mother, her self-hatred transformed into my own through the alchemy of abuse.

So when Bill Shirer tries to take my picture I'm terrified. He's always hovering around me with a camera but I cover my face with my hands, duck to get out of the way. I'm like those aborigines who think the camera steals your soul, except I think the camera will expose my soul, my essential unlovability, show me for who I am, someone who is nothing like the person he thinks I am. Never for a moment do I consider the possibility that he *is* really seeing me, that he could love me for myself, even though another part of me has become accustomed to, even learned to take for granted, his affectionate esteem.

I can smile, I can make myself look pretty and shiny, I can pretend to be who he thinks I am and convince him and even myself, sort of, that I am who he thinks I am. But if he takes a picture of me, a representation of myself that I can't fake and have no control over, the ugliness in me will be captured and exposed in a permanent way—the photo of me sitting on his mantel among the others he has there, people coming here and seeing it, him looking at it whenever he wants.

Finally, because he won't stop insisting that I let him take a picture of me, I tell him I'll bring one for him the next time I come. This is not ideal but at least I have some control over the image. I go back home and ask my friend, an amateur professional photographer with a good Nikon, to take some photos of me. She and I go to a park. She tells me to sit on a bench, turn sideways, bend my knees, put my feet up on the end of the seat, and turn to the camera, and she takes a bunch of black-and-white photos of me. Black and white is my choice; I look even worse in color.

I still have one of those pictures. It shows a young woman with blond hair slumping slightly on a park bench, smiling into the camera. She is cute, even pretty, I can see that now. Even then I liked the batch of photos enough to feel okay about giving one to Bill Shirer. Bill was disappointed. He really wanted a color picture instead of a black-and-white one, and he wanted one or a bunch of ones that he had taken himself. But he accepted the photo I gave him and put it on his mantel.

I must've spent twenty weekends with him over a period of about three years. I went to Tanglewood with him and sat on a blanket under the oak trees and listened to Mahler's ninth symphony. We had a picnic lunch there and when the concert was over, as he was driving back across the lawn, he went just a little too fast, the car hit a dip in the grass and bounced and I hit my head on the ceiling. "I'm sorry, I'm sorry," he said over and over, and I could see he really was, sorry he had made a mistake, sorry he was inadequate and let the car get out of control, sorry I had hit my head. Once when we were coming back to his house, a little drunk after going out to dinner, we saw a skunk by the front door; it disappeared behind the metal milk box on the step. That was in the early days, when he could still drink—eventually he had to give it up, and give up driving too, but I was gone by the time that happened.

He had a delicate heart, had had heart surgery during the 1960s after a heart attack, although it didn't seem to slow him down or worry him in any way. Once when I arrived and he met me at the bus stop, I could feel his heart flipping and fluttering like a small bird inside his chest when he pulled me to him for a hug. I knew that was happening because of me—that his heart was beating fast the way mine did when I saw some man I fancied myself in love with—but I didn't want to think about it. And once he used the word "ardent" to describe our interaction when we first connected at the bus stop; I didn't want to think about that either. I was embarrassed by the suggestion that he and I were ardent. I wasn't ardent but he was and that was embarrassing, or maybe it just made me uncomfortable to imagine whatever he was imagining about me.

Once, on a warm blue Saturday afternoon, he drove me to a lake in Lenox and tried to teach me how to sail. He had been sailing since his days in Connecticut after the war and he had his own sailboat which he kept tied up in a dock at the lake. I wore my swimsuit under my clothes and stripped down to it nervously on the grass by the water. None of this was something

I normally did back then or was comfortable doing. Along with feeling invisible and being afraid to speak in public during this part of my life, I believed in the deepest heart of my heart that I was somehow different from other people, that I couldn't do the ordinary things that other people did, sailing or swimming in lakes or flying on airplanes. Certainly I didn't feel comfortable being almost naked in the sunshine in the presence of a famous old man who thought he loved me although he didn't really know me at all or at least so I thought. Standing there on the grass in my bathing suit, waiting to get into the boat, I felt white and exposed, even ugly, but Bill Shirer smiled fondly at me as if he thought I was beautiful, as if this was another notable moment in his long life full of notable moments.

The other day I looked him up on Google. There was the standard Wikipedia article, a couple of websites with quotes by William Shirer and one called Pronunciation of Shirer. At first I misread it as Pronouncements of Shirer, and I thought how much he would have loved having a website featuring his pronouncements. He wouldn't have loved it because he had an inflated ego, as someone I know suggested. Bill didn't have an inflated ego. He was almost apologetic, a little embarrassed, about his standing and status, and underneath that was humility in the true sense of the word: He knew who and what he was and he didn't have to try to be more or less than it.

He would have appreciated a Pronouncements of William Shirer website because he often made pronouncements and it was important to him that his pronouncements be heard and heeded by as many people as possible. He was outraged by racism, fascism, oppression, things that were wrong in the world. And he was stubborn in his outrage. He would not shut up about the Nazis, watching and recording their rise to power in the 1930s when nobody in the world, not even the U.S. government, was paying much attention; sneaking out messages about the Third Reich when he could have been arrested by the Nazis for doing it, during the 1940s; writing that book, *The Rise and Fall of the Third Reich*, for more than a decade to make sure nobody forgot the lessons to be learned from Nazi Germany. Starting in the 1960s, until the end of his life, he refused to forgive William R. Murrow, his broadcasting partner in Nazi Germany—they did the first world news round-up in 1938 after Hitler invaded Austria—because in 1964 Murrow refused to stand up for him when he lost his job at CBS. When I knew Bill, the magazine "Modern Maturity" asked him to write an essay about what he thought were the biggest stories of the 20th century. They probably expected some nostalgic retrospective from an old guy who remembered firsthand, but instead he wrote a blistering piece about the threat of nuclear war and the dangers of nuclear power.

He hated Ronald Reagan. He even suggested a couple of times there was something Hitleresque about the way Reagan spoke to crowds and curried favor with the right wing by twisting the truth. I can't imagine what he would have done with Donald Trump in office. Actually, I can imagine it, and I wish he was here to do it. I wish he was still alive to make some more of his stubborn, tough-minded, uncompromising pronouncements—to say more things like this, which I found when I clicked on the link for quotes from William L. Shirer: "Perhaps America will one day go fascist democratically, by popular vote."

I'm remembering that letter on top of the gray file cabinet in Bill's guest room, me standing there trying to make sense of it back in the early 1980s. I know now that Bill was blacklisted in the 1950s. His name appeared along with 150 others in a publication called Red Channels, because he had been on an anti-fascist, pro-Republican committee in Spain, and because he had signed a document along with many others asking the U.S. Supreme Court to administer justice in the case of the ten movie producers, directors, and screenplay writers who received jail sentences and were banned from working because they refused to testify before the House Un-American Activities Committee. For signing that document and being on that committee, he was deemed suspicious of having Communist sympathies although he didn't and there was no way for him to defend himself although he tried. When he was barred from working in the broadcast industry for ten years, he wrote *The Rise and Fall of the Third Reich*, which turned out to be one of the bestselling books of all times. But during those ten years when he was writing it, as he often told me, he had no real source of income and his wife left him because he wouldn't support the family.

I'm thinking about the Nazis, Joseph McCarthy, Roy Cohn—McCarthy's advisor and henchman and later Donald Trump's mentor and lawyer—and Donald Trump, how they're all linked together like images in a dot-to-dot picture of history. It's interesting to me that Bill Shirer, who was a chief witness and chronicler of the Nazis, in another decade came under the damaging scrutiny of Joseph McCarthy's Communist witch hunt; how Roy Cohn, in yet another decade, met and mentored Donald Trump, infected him or confirmed in him a particular style of self-promotion: insulting others, never admitting the slightest wrongdoing, twisting the truth. Bill Shirer and Adolf Hitler and Joseph McCarthy and Roy Cohn are all gone; Ethel and Julius Rosenberg died in the electric chair so long ago hardly anybody remembers them. But Donald Trump was recently our 45th president, like history looping back upon itself, the political crimes of the past folded inside the current moment like clues in a set of Chinese boxes. I think of how the past is hidden inside the present, the way the old versions of myself—the young woman whose photo sat on Bill Shirer's mantel, who was afraid to be seen, who was carrying her own hidden traumas of the past—are still inside me.


In 1986 I was admitted to the Iowa Writers' Workshop and moved to Iowa City. Bill was sad that I was moving away but he also thought it was an amusing coincidence that I was moving to Iowa, because he had grown up in Cedar Rapids near Iowa City and I grew up in Western Massachusetts near Lenox where he lived now. He kept saying we had switched places. After I moved he called me now and then and once he came out to Iowa to visit his alma mater, Coe College in Cedar Rapids, and also, as he told me in his affectionate way on the phone, to see me. I drove him to his old college and walked across the grass with him and the college president. The president pointed to a fraternity house and asked Bill if he wanted to stop by there and say hi to some of the boys and Bill said, "No, I'm not a fraternity kind of guy." He and I had dinner in Iowa City that night, and afterwards, upstairs in his hotel room, we stood gazing out the window at the lights of Iowa City and he said in a dreamy voice, "Everything looks different when you're away from home."

He died in 1993, a few weeks shy of his ninetieth birthday. He always said that when the time came for his life to be over he wanted to step away from the table graciously so others could take their places. But his daughter told me on the phone that his death wasn't easy and he didn't particularly want to go. And I sense that if he could be somewhere now, looking down from the afterlife, he might not be so happy to be forced to take a backseat, to not get to be an actor in this twenty-first century, Donald Trump and all.

I was sad when Bill died but I went on with my life and after a while I stopped thinking about him; I didn't think about him very much for a long time. Then the other day I was going through my bookshelves and came across my copies of his books, each of which he gave me with an inscription in his spidery old-man literary-looking handwriting:  The Pocket Books paperback edition of *Gandhi: A Memoir,* first published by Simon & Shuster in 1979, and all three volumes of *20th Century Journey: A Memoir of a Life and the Times.* The second volume, *The Nightmare Years, 1930-1940,* is the one I worked on at Little, Brown. The third volume, *A Native's Return, 1945-1988,* is inscribed, "To Mary—the last work, I promise! about me. With admiration and love, Xmas 1989." I was living in Iowa by then and he sent it to me in a jiffy bag for Christmas.

I look at those books now and think about how nobody's reading them anymore. I think of how all that history, all that living, are over. Even books in general, not writing but the physical objects themselves with their covers and pages, are almost over. And Bill himself, of course, is no longer here. Time barrels along into the future without him, the present rapidly becoming the past, the news turning into history. Everything we count on and everything we engage in, the very fabric of our lives and the scaffolding we nail it to, all gone or departing or constantly changing, even the nightmare years.

# Cowboy Justice

It's November 1, 1991, an ordinary Friday afternoon, the day after Halloween. I'm behind a desk in a big office on the fifth floor of Van Allen Hall, where the Physics Department at the University of Iowa is housed, when I hear a noise on a floor below: *Pop pop pop.* That sounds like gunshots, I think. But this is many years before school shootings, mass shootings of all sorts, have become so common they're the first thing you think of when you hear a sound like a gun going off. And so I decide that what I heard must have been a staple gun, that they must be doing construction down there. This seems plausible, especially because after the *pop pop pop* I hear what sounds like heavy furniture being rearranged. Later on I'll learn that this was the sound of people scrambling to get under desks and shoving tables aside as they rushed out the door.

But at the moment I don't have a clue what's going on and I just sit there at my desk and continue working, printing out labels and attaching them to envelopes and folding a little pile of letters signed by my boss, Christoph Goertz, editor of the Journal of Geophysical Research, before he left for the Friday afternoon theoretical space physics meeting downstairs where he has just been shot along with two other people. When I finish sealing the envelopes I go down a long dark hallway to the bathroom where I use the facilities and stare at myself in the mirror, then stop at the water fountain outside the bathroom door and fill a little plastic tube with a removable pink sponge on the end, which I plan to use to seal the envelopes containing the letters from Chris Goertz.

As I'm wandering back down the hall to my office a young woman, a secretary I know, appears at the top of the stairwell and says, *Dwight's been shot! He's dead.*

*Did they catch the guy who did it?* I ask her.

*I don't think so*, she says. And then she says, *I think it was that guy Gang Lu*, turns around, and heads back down the stairs.

Dwight is Dwight Nicholson, the chairman of the Physics Department, who, I will later learn, was shot in the back by the gunman while he was peacefully working at his desk facing the wall. The gunman was indeed that guy Gang Lu, a recent Ph.D. recipient who was angry his thesis didn't get an award he thought would increase his chances of getting a job and not having to return to post-Tiananmen-Square China. After he killed Dwight he went back up upstairs to the meeting room where a few minutes earlier he shot Chris Goertz and two other people: Bob Smith, another professor, and Linhua Shan, the young man who won the award he didn't win. Chris and Shan died immediately—Chris was the first victim, shot in the head at close range at the front of the room; in the first few seconds, before reality sank in, some people thought it was a Halloween prank—but Bob Smith was only wounded.

Two men were kneeling on the floor beside Bob when the gunman came back. Gang Lu told them to leave the room and then he shot Bob again, finishing the job. Then he left the building, walked over to a university administration building and killed Anne Cleary, the university's grievance officer, who had not responded favorably to his complaint about not receiving the award. He also shot Miya Rodolfo-Sioson, a first-day temp worker who just happened to get in the way. She was an activist, a dancer, a beautiful spirit, as we all learned later, the only survivor and Gang Lu's only impromptu victim. She spent the rest of her short life in a wheelchair, paralyzed from the neck down. Afterwards Gang Lu found an empty classroom on the second floor, took off his tan jacket and folded it neatly over the back of a chair, and shot himself in the head.

We know all these details now; they've been public knowledge for more than thirty years. They pale in comparison to the horrors inflicted by other mass gunmen in the years since then—the random slaughter of innocent children, teachers, school administrators, people in nightclubs, churches, movies, concert halls, casinos, suburban malls—the devastation of families, the trauma of the survivors. But this is only the second school shooting, the first if you don't count Charles Whitman shooting from a tower at the University of Texas in 1966, and nobody is prepared for it or knows what to make of it—not that it would help anything if we were or did.

I go back to my office and call my friend Jo Ann, who shares this job with me. Her line is busy, so I hang up and sit there wondering what to do. There is nothing to do, so I just keep working, sealing the envelopes containing the letters that will never be sent. I'm confused instead of scared. I'm too confused to be scared. I don't close the door, I don't do anything about the fact that there could be a murderer somewhere in the building.

I seal a few more envelopes, then I get up and stand in the doorway, looking down the hall. I see a Chinese student with a backpack emerge from the stairwell and I run back into my office. Nothing happens—the shooter is over in the other building by now; he is not that guy with the backpack, although I don't know that. I sit down at the desk and try to call Jo Ann again. This time she answers and I tell her that Dwight's been shot and he's dead and she's shocked and stunned. We don't even know yet that there are other victims, people we work with directly; she knows them better than I do—I was hired four months ago but she's been working here for years—one of them is our boss. She tells me to close the door of the office.

I do and we talk some more. Then someone comes running down the hall, pounding on doors and yelling, "Everyone get out of the building! They're evacuating the building!"

I hang up in a hurry, look around, and find myself in a quandary. Later on I'll look back on this moment as evidence of what an embarrassingly obedient, good girl I was back then. It probably does show that, but it's also further evidence of how jarring and bewildering, how mindboggling it is to be lifted suddenly out of ordinary life and thrust into a life-threatening crisis, how it takes a while to make the mental leap from one to the other. My quandary is, I can't figure out whether to turn off the business machines. It's Friday, I think, they'll be running all weekend and probably longer, maybe they'll overheat or something, and I decide to turn them off.

I go all around the room, turning off the postal meter, the copy machine, the computer, the printer. My hands are shaking so hard I can hardly press the buttons, and that's when I realize, the first time I realize, how scared I am. I walk down the long dark fifth-floor hallway to the elevator. All the doors are closed and I don't see anyone, there's no one to share this terrifying moment with. I step into the elevator and ride alone to the first floor. The whole way down I worry that the elevator will stop and a graduate student with a backpack full of guns will get on. That doesn't happen, and I get out of the elevator on the first floor, where I see flashing lights beyond the exit and policemen by the door waving guns and shouting, *Everyone out! Out of the building!*

It's snowing outside, large white flakes whirling madly in the air. I don't have a car, and during my entire twenty-minute walk home, up a long straight sloping tree-lined street, I feel like a murderer is following me.

When I get home I call Jo Ann, she picks me up and drives me to her house, and we sit around anxiously, saying the same things over and over, with a few other friends.  News drifts in over the radio.  By ten o'clock we know that five people are dead and someone was wounded but is still alive. We know the shooting involved Chris Goertz's Friday afternoon meeting on the third floor of Van Allen Hall, that people we know, people Jo Ann has worked with for years, are probably dead.  But we're still holding out hope that Chris Goertz, our boss and friend, isn't dead.  Maybe he's the one survivor, maybe somehow there's been a mistake.  Jo Ann and I bargain.  *Okay*, we say, *Dwight is dead, we know that for sure.  Bob Smith can be dead.  But please, please don't let it be Chris.*  The ten o'clock news comes on, they briefly tell the story and prepare to announce the victims.  The first face that appears on the screen is Chris Goertz's face.

The aftermath is more or less predictable.  There are memorial services, articles in the paper and then editorials, the whole community grieves.  Everybody talks about where they were when the shooting happened.  Things come out about Gang Lu.  He bought his gun at Fin and Feather and did target practicing for months.  He wrote a long rambly letter to his sister in China, single-spaced on white typing paper, and mailed it the day of the shooting.  It was intercepted by the authorities at the Iowa City post office; he tells his sister not to be sad for him because he'll be quantum leaping through the universe (at the time there was a show on TV called Quantum Leap) and he's going to take a few traveling companions with him.  On an old Greyhound-bus-ticket envelope the police found in his apartment, he had scrawled, "Cowboy justice is the only action against corporate crime."

People continue writing editorials, many of them speculating about why something like this happened.  There's talk in some circles about how hard life is for graduate students, suggesting that Gang Lu was pushed to his limits by the pressures of academia. A group of us forms to take action on gun control and we meet for about a year. In 2009 a movie is made loosely based on the story; it shifts the onus of the bad guy onto the graduate-advisor Chris Goertz character and casts the Gang Lu character in the role of the underdog. I write a letter to the editor of the *LA Times* trying to set the record straight. On the twentieth anniversary of the shooting, a local reporter interviews me as someone who was there. When I tell Jo Ann about the upcoming interview she tells me what I haven't heard anyone say before: The very people Gang Lu killed in a fit of rage and madness and victim mentality, the people he blamed for causing his problems, were trying to *help* him. Chris and Dwight both thought he was brilliant and were sure he would get a job; Chris had written him a glowing recommendation Jo Ann found post-mortem in Chris's desk. I say this in the interview and it gets aired on the local ten o'clock news, but it's probably too late for it to matter to anyone but me and Jo Ann and friends and family members of the victims.

The whole story is rife with misunderstandings. Gang Lu thought Chris ignored his thesis in favor of Linhua Shan's: Chris actually recommended both theses for the award and an outside award committee made the choice. Gang Lu told the grievance officer, Anne Cleary, that the UI space physics group had unfairly passed him over for the award; Anne Cleary didn't do anything because Chris reported that Gang Lu had been recommended for the award. I had to rewrite this piece twice because, as I learned when I started researching, I remembered a lot of the details wrong.

What are we to learn from all this? What did I learn from it? I learned that the truth is subject to shape-shifting and misinterpretation, that the farther you are from a public event the more mythical proportions it assumes, that popular mythology—the illusion of cowboy justice, for instance—can be deadly, that there is no rational reason for murder. And that in a country where anyone can buy a gun in a store, blame, hate, distorted thinking, misunderstandings, and—almost certainly—mental illness, can lead to the mass slaughter of ordinary people.

# The Way Back Home

I'm on an Amtrak train, coming back to Iowa City from Ithaca, where I've been visiting my friend Jo Ann. The train is approaching Chicago, and there's a fourteen-year-old boy in the seat beside me. We'll never see each other again but we've established a kind of friendly joking relationship; he's cute in a fourteen-year-old-boy sort of way, clean cut with short brown hair and a relaxed pleasant respectful-enough manner. He taught me how to play pinochle and we've been playing and I've even won a few games.

I decide to go to the bathroom and put some lipstick on before we get to Chicago. There's going to be a three-hour layover there, so I get up and make my way along the aisle between the seats, grabbing hold of one seat-back after another as I move along so as not to be thrown off balance by the train's bumping and shifting and shuttling. I go into the little bathroom on the left side of the aisle where the passenger seats end, push across the lock so it will say occupied, warning off anyone who wants to come in, put my purse down on a shelf under a little mirror, and turn to the little toilet. There's something smeared all over the seat and suddenly I smell what it is—it's *shit*. Then I register with a shock that there appears to be shit all over where it shouldn't be in this little bathroom: on the toilet, on the sink, on the shelf I've placed my bag on, and I grab my purse and run out.

There's another bathroom directly across from the one I've just left and I'm relieved when I go in there and see that that the little toilet seat is clean, everything looks clean. I use that bathroom and then go back down the shifting, shuttling aisle to my seat.

"There was shit in there all over the toilet," I say to the boy in the seat beside me.

"Oh yeah?" he says. He doesn't seem remotely interested, as if shit on a toilet is an ordinary thing and there's something inappropriate about making a big deal about it. But I still feel shocked, and I sit there wondering how that shit got on there like that, wondering who would do such a thing and why. I can still smell it too, and at first I think it must just be the memory of what I smelled in the bathroom that I'm smelling. I look down at the front of my shirt and there's something dark brown and greasy looking on it. I briefly consider the possibility that this might be candy which I've somehow gotten on my shirt without noticing—have I been eating chocolate while I was playing pinochle and somehow forgotten? Still in a state of denial and disbelief I lift the fabric of my shirt and sniff and a shockwave of shit odor rolls over me again. I realize that I was holding my leather purse to my chest when I was walking back down the aisle and I reach down and pick my purse up off the floor between my feet, sniff the bottom of it, and oh my God it's there too.

"I have to go to the bathroom and wash off my purse," I say to the boy, who's reading a paperback science fiction novel now. He barely looks up and nods before disappearing into his reading again. I go to the clean bathroom and wash my hands under the little dribbling faucet, pushing the button on the liquid soap dispenser over and over. I wet a paper towel and put soap on it and try to clean off the bottom of my purse and then use several other paper towels to try to get the shit off the front of my shirt.

Back in my seat I still smell shit, but I feel fairly confident that I've gotten most of it off my purse, at least. Then, gradually, another idea dawns on me. My off-white canvas bag containing my library book is on the floor at my feet, it's been down there all the time, beside my purse. I slowly pick it up and bring it to my nose. Oh surely not this too, I think, feeling fairly confident that I'm just being paranoid. I sniff the bag and realize with an overwhelming sense of betrayal that nothing is safe in this moment, my purse, my shirt, my hands, and now my canvas bag are all tainted with shit.

I go back to the bathroom, carrying my shitty purse and the canvas bag, and I spend at least ten minutes there washing my hands, washing the bottom of both bags, in the little sink in that tiny enclosed room. Afterwards I can still smell the not-even-faint smell of shit on all three things, and as I walk back down the aisle to my seat I feel sort of soiled and tainted myself, as if the shit I can't get off my hands, my purse, my bag, my shirt, is somehow my shit, and it's not just shit but something that means something about me. I scan the faces of the other passengers, searching for evidence of shit exposure, for looks of shame and panic on any of them, but they all look back at me blankly, with normal, bland, bored or in a few cases mildly interested expressions, and I see that I'm alone in this, I'm the only one with shit on them. I've been made separate from all the other people on this train, more separate than I already felt, because there's shit on me.

I go to the McDonald's in the train station in Chicago and buy a white t-shirt with Ronald McDonald emblazoned on the front. I take the t-shirt to the train station restroom, rip off the shirt I've been wearing, wad it up, and throw it in the trashcan. I pull my new shirt over my head, and then I spend the rest of the entire three-hour layover standing at the sink, washing the bottom of my purse, washing my canvas bag, washing my hands. Still, when I sniff my fingers as we board the train again, it's still there, a lot fainter than it was before but nevertheless unmistakable.

The boy is already in his seat when I get to mine. I put my purse and canvas bag on the metal shelf rack above the seats—who knows what's on the floor.

"It won't wash off," I say to the boy after I've settled in and the train has started moving. "I can't believe how hard it is to get rid of the smell of shit."

The boy shrugs and turns his face to the window.

"*I have shit on me!*" I say a little hysterically. The boy shrugs again and continues looking out the window, and in that moment something in me caves in and goes ahead and just accepts it: I have shit on me and there's nothing I can do about it, and I'm going to have to sit here in this seat for another four hours, smelling like shit, feeling like shit, and that's all there is to it.

And then I have another thought.

Because I've started going to a twelve-step program for family members and friends of alcoholics and the idea of being affected by someone else's problems is never far from my mind, because I believe that whatever happens to you happens for a reason, I decide to ask Life, the universe, my higher power, to show me what the shit on the train is really about. I do, and the answer springs instantly into my mind: This is why I'm going to those twelve-step meetings, this is what I'm suffering from which might just be life: Somebody else's shit gets on you and you can't get it off.

# At the Monastery

Last summer at New Melleray Abbey I saw a monk who reminded me of my late fiancé, Jim Beaman. It was during Compline, the last canonical hour of the day.

During Compline at New Melleray, four black-and-white-robed monks come out and stand in the middle of the floor; one of them plays the guitar and all four of them sing, in harmony, the 91$^{st}$ psalm. It's always the same.

All the hours services are the same, although the psalms they sing at the other services vary according to the day of the week and whether it's an odd or an even week. But they always sing the 91$^{st}$ psalm during Compline, and it's always the same monks who sing it and the same monk who plays the guitar, and it always sounds the same although somehow it manages to be fresh and new and startlingly beautiful every single time, those four monks' voices rising and falling in a strange haunting harmony.

I've been going to New Melleray, a Trappist monastery in Northeast Iowa, once or twice a year since the summer of 1994, when I was struggling with a writing problem and somebody told me it was a good place to get away and think. Most recently I spent two days there with my friend Mary, who'd come to Iowa City from Ft. Collins, Colorado, to attend a weeklong writing class I taught at our local university. Up until that moment during Compline last summer, I'd never paid much attention to the guitar-playing monk.

When I was up there with Mary, I noticed that the monk who plays the guitar during Compline was short and young and cute—at least I imagined he was cute, looking at the back of him from a fairly good distance—and he had close-cropped brown hair and wire-rimmed glasses, all of which Jim Beaman had or was. Even more than his appearance, there was something boyish and maybe a little rebellious looking about him that made me think of Beaman. And even more than that, I remembered as I was sitting there at the back of the chapel, there was something about Jim Beaman that reminded me of that monk, something about Beaman that made you think he could have, if he had managed to live an entirely different life, ended up in some monastery playing the guitar and singing the 91$^{st}$ psalm.

During Compline, after the guitar-playing and the singing, the four monks walk humbly with their heads down back to their seats—the monks sit in two rows of stalls that face each other across the chapel floor; the guests sit on wooden benches at the back, cordoned off behind a black wrought-iron fence—and there's a period of silence. Compline takes place at 7:30 p.m. If it's summertime and the windows are open and the days are long, as it was the last time I was at the monastery, you can hear birds singing and an occasional truck downshifting on the road in the distance, you can hear the tired dusty hum of the world still going on outside that silent space; there are wide bands of yellow late-day sunlight along the edges of the benches in the guest section, swatches of sunlight on the floor on one side of the chapel where the monks sit. But if it's wintertime the entire place is dark, except for the little wavering sanctuary light all the way at the front of the chapel. Whether it's dark and silent or light and full of airiness and silent you sit there in the silence, unbroken except for an occasional cough or sound of someone shifting in his seat, for seven minutes or so. And then the enormous bell in the bell tower outside the chapel rings slowly nine times in three sets of three—dong dong dong, dong dong dong, dong dong dong—and then it rings three much longer rings: donnnnggg, donnnnggg, donnnngggggg.

And then after a little while they turn the lights back on and two monks get up and stand in the middle of floor. The other monks queue up in front of them in two parallel lines and one of the monks at the front waves an instrument containing holy water and each monk bows his head when he gets to the head of the line and receives a drop or two of holy water to keep him safe from the forces of darkness during the night. When the monks are almost finished getting their holy water, the guest-master monk comes and opens a gate in the wrought-iron fence that separates the guests from the chapel and says, in a quiet peaceful voice: "If you'd like to come up front for a blessing you're welcome." And then all of us in the back file forward and get in one of the two parallel lines to receive our drop of holy water.

You don't always get some. Sometimes the water misses and falls to the floor. I've determined through trial and error that if you're in the line on the right you have a better chance of getting holy water than if you're on the left. Even so, and even though I try to stand still at just the right distance from the monk with the holy water, I still occasionally come away dry or with only a drop on my shirt sleeve where I can't feel it. I like to get a good splat right on the face or the head. I don't know exactly what holy water is supposed to do, I don't even know how to make the sign of the cross, but somehow I always feel a little bit safer, a little bit cleaner and purer and happier, walking away with that water on me.

Jim Beaman would have known all about holy water. Once, when he was a kid of nine or ten, serving as an altar boy in Bettendorf, Iowa, he and a friend drank some of the communion wine in the sacristy, then found out it had already been blessed. It seemed like a terrible sin—later he had to confess and receive a penance—but I always thought there was an aura of something a little bit holy about him, some lingering purity or innocence or magic, and it pleased me to entertain the idea that it had something to do with that wine. I never thought it could have acted as a curse—that was his joke about it—although it is true without a doubt that wine, beer, and other kinds of alcohol contributed heavily to the ruining of his life. So maybe it was somehow symbolic of what was to come, that moment in the sacristy when he and his boyhood buddy took that fateful swig out of the chalice.

"Jim Beaman was a Catholic," I told my friend Mary at the monastery, as we were climbing the stairs after lunch, going to the third floor where our rooms were, the day after I noticed the monk who reminded me of Beaman during Compline.

"Oh really?" said Mary, looking interested like the good friend she is. "I didn't know that." Like most of my friends, she's never met Jim Beaman, has just heard me talk about him occasionally over the years.

"Yes," I said. "He even mentioned it in his suicide note. I always thought it had something to do with why he killed himself."

Mary looked at me as if she was about to say something, then another retreatant, an elderly woman we had gotten friendly with during our stay, came down the stairs and started talking to us and Mary and I lost the thread of that conversation and never picked it up again. But I thought about it as I was lying on my bed staring at the recessed light fixture in the ceiling of my room that afternoon.

When you stay at the monastery you get your own little room and your own bathroom. The room has a single bed with clean white sheets, a wool blanket, and a tan polyester bedspread; it also has a wooden desk and chair, another more comfortable chair in the corner, and a little wooden footstool. Some of the rooms face inside onto the courtyard and some of them face out onto the parked cars and the lawn. There's a scattering of leafy trees on the lawn and a few picnic tables and white-painted wooden lawn chairs; there are flowerbeds as well, and in the middle of the lawn is a marble statue of the Virgin Mary which glows at night; I could see it—her—out my window the last time I stayed at the monastery. There are also wooden boxes on pedestals, sort of like birdhouses or possibly small dollhouses, set at intervals around the periphery of the lawn. Riveted onto each is a laminated, metal-framed, black-and-white picture depicting one of the stations of the cross: Jesus taking up the cross, falling three times under the burden of the cross, being stripped, being nailed to the cross, dying on the cross.

I don't understand the appeal of all that. When I was thirteen years old I joined the Congregational church in Westhampton, Massachusetts, and I've barely gone to church since. It makes me queasy to look at the pictures on those boxes. But I do like the statue of the blessed Virgin, staring mildly and with great compassion at the leaves and grass at her feet out there in the middle of the abbey's lawn.

Mostly what you do when you're at the monastery is stay in your room alone and lie on your bed and look at the ceiling or sit in the chair by the window and stare out at the lawn or the courtyard or read or go for little walks by yourself. Time goes slowly at the monastery, at least twice as slowly as it goes anywhere else. The afternoons are endless, from 12:30 when lunch is over to 5:30 when Vespers and then supper take place—there's None at 1:45 but I never go to that. And when you're lying on your bed staring up at the ceiling, no email, no phone calls, no errands, no money worries, no chores or pets or needs and wants of other people to distract and annoy and make you anxious, time stretches out before you vast and empty, like an enormous snowy field. You have all the time you could ever need and then some to nap and read, to think and not think. And as I was lying on my bed the day after the evening I noticed that monk during Compline, I remembered a Sunday morning when I was lying next to Jim Beaman in his room on his single bed, the sheets dirty and rumpled, both of us for different reasons dirty and rumpled, tired, stretched to the limit of our endurance by the last few days, and he looked over at me and said with great pain and bitterness, "It's Sunday morning and we're going to go to church."

He had never said anything like that, had never even said the word church to me unless it figured in a story or two about growing up Catholic, until that day.

It's hard for me to go back to the place he and I were in that Sunday morning about eighteen years ago. I'm not talking about the physical place so much as the spiritual circumstances of where we were then, far, far away from the spiritual aura of a monastery or a church, which of course was the source of Beaman's bitterness, the irony, the admission of fault and guilt. I remember looking over at him and noticing that he wasn't looking at me, noticing the way his hair stuck up at the back of his head, the miserable, stubborn, hell-bent look on his face. Shortly after that he got up and sat at the desk and started messing around with the needles, the spoon, the cigarette lighter, going back to what he'd been doing pretty much steadily for about 48 hours, and at that point I said, "I can't take any more of this," and left, walked the short block to my own apartment, sat in the pink chair in my living room and started making phone calls. Calling his friend John Gray to see if there was anything he could do to help him—"Absolutely not," he said. "He's been pulling this shit for years and I've given up trying to help him"—calling my friend Kathy to try to get help for myself.

Later on, after it was all over and I was taking Beaman to the hospital with blood poisoning and he was sober, repentant, ready once again to try to turn his life around, he said to me, "Yesterday I thought I was going to go somewhere, somewhere really bad, but I've changed my mind."

I was just so relieved that he was getting sober—forever, once and for all, I stupidly thought, as if he could have done that—so relieved that he was sticking around instead of going somewhere, I didn't ask him where it was he'd thought of going; it didn't occur to me to wonder what he'd meant by somewhere really bad because he was already somewhere really bad. I was only happy that at that moment we were going somewhere better, even if it was a hospital where he could recover. It was only much later that I understood what he was saying, understood where—what—that really bad place was, understood after he ended up going there after all about six months later, and knew that it was a place he had been preparing to go to since the early days of his Catholic childhood. Among the things he left behind was an autograph book from our Lady of Lourdes grammar school. There were the usual comments about girls who liked him and his good sense of humor, but I was struck by one, unsigned and written in a boy's messy fourth-grade handwriting, that said, "To Jim, See you in hell."


There was a monk among the students in the class I taught recently. Brother Francis is in his fifties and lives in St. Meinrad's in Indiana. During my class he said that living in a monastery is a lot different from being a visitor in a monastery, that monastic living versus visiting is sort of like being in a marriage compared to experiencing the first blush of romance. I wish I had gotten him to say more about that because I've always been deeply curious about what it would be like to live the monastic life, what it would be like to know you were going to do the same things over and over, day in and day out, to devote yourself to prayer and meditation, to doing the work you were given to do—the monks at New Melleray farm and build caskets, Brother Francis works at a press—and do it solely for the sake of itself and nothing else.

And in the same idle way, I've wondered what it would have been like if Jim Beaman had lived and we had actually gotten married. Somehow I knew all along that we never would; I knew it was just a fantasy even as I was collaborating in it, although I never thought it would all end the way it did and I couldn't imagine it ending any other way either. But still, I sometimes like to think about what it would have been like if he had gotten sober and we had both attended twelve-step programs and together made an ordinary life, engaging in the every-day struggles of living and growing together, trying to communicate and accept each other's shortcomings and do the other hard work of any marriage which, I guess, is similar to the hard work it takes, according to Brother Francis, to live with others in a monastery.

The monk who reminded me of Jim Beaman was wearing black shoes—I noticed the shoes during Compline on the second day of last summer's stay at the monastery. I caught a glimpse of his face then too and thought I saw nice lips, deep-set eyes, other features that resembled Jim Beaman's, but the truth is all I really saw clearly were those shoes. That and his straight back in the robe, his way of holding the guitar out in front of him as he strums the simple tune that goes with the words of the 91st psalm, night after night during Compline, the way he sways a little when he plays. The other three monks who stand in the middle of the chapel floor, singing to his accompaniment, all wear simple hemp sandals, the kind you associate with Jesus and other ascetic types; one of those monks is tall, narrow, and relatively young, with a longish beard and longish hair. It's not hard to imagine him having a checkered past—you can see in his face the traces of a rebellious streak that hasn't quite gone into remission—and I'm sure there are others at the monastery who had turbulent lives before becoming monks. I like to think that the monk who looks like Jim Beaman, the monk with the guitar and the black shoes—shoes that look incongruous, overly formal, even inappropriate at the bottom of a pair of jeans showing at the bottom of a long black-and-white belted robe—I like to think that he, like Jim Beaman, has had his share of struggles, that he might have fought with demons and unlike Beaman won.

After Jim Beaman died I read somewhere that you should pray for the dead, pray the words of the Hail Mary with a rosary, that this will help the dead in some powerful indefinable way. And so I did that. I didn't get a rosary but I asked someone I knew who was Catholic to tell me the words of the Hail Mary and I memorized them and said them over and over, mostly in bed at night before I went to sleep: *Hail Mary, full of grace, the lord is with thee, blessed art thou among women and blessed is the fruit of thy womb, Jesus. Holy Mary, mother of God, pray for us sinners now and at the hour of our death.* Every night, many nights in a row, I said those words over and over until I was almost asleep, until I was in and out of sleep and still saying those words, the image of Jim Beaman at the hour of his death at the edge of my consciousness like a dark, terrible dream.

In waking life I kept imagining him sitting at his desk during that hour, that moment, holding the gun in his lap and pointing it at his head. But then his roommate told me that he was lying on his bed when he did it, and for some reason that really bothered me. I'm sure it was partly because of all the other associations I had with his bed, not the awful morning with the rumpled covers and the stuff laid out on the desk, which was just a precursor and therefore more or less interchangeable with the final act that took place on that bed, but good moments on other days when we were lying there together napping, talking, laughing, and, of course, although most often we did this at my house in a different bed—having sex. It was troubling to have the image of the suicide, something so evil and unimaginable it didn't even seem to belong to this world, superimposed forever on top of that other normal happy stuff. But it was also the specificity of the image I conjured up whenever I thought of him doing it on the bed—the fact that I could so easily *see* him there, doing that—that made it horrible.

He did leave that note, and when I first heard about it but before I had read it —the note was held by the police for a few days, along with Beaman's diary and a few other things—I felt a momentary breath of relief, as if the note was going to explain everything and that would somehow make things better. But in the end the note was almost unreadable. There were just partial sentences, scribbled in the messy illegible handwriting of someone who was obviously far under the influence, you could almost hear his thoughts trailing off. One of the unfinished sentences was, *To my Catholic… I know I'm …*

How would he have finished that sentence if he had been anywhere near his right mind, I've often wondered. Would he have mentioned sin, hell, grace, forgiveness?

*May the souls of the faithful departed, in the mercy of God, rest in peace,* one of the monks at New Melleray intones every day, in a deep sonorous slightly nasal voice, at the end of one of the offices. Whenever I hear that I think of Jim Beaman. I wonder whether the Catholic church would consider him one of the faithful departed and decide that they wouldn't, and then I wonder whether that matters at all, even on the deepest of spiritual levels, and decide it doesn't. I wonder whether

Jim Beaman, faithful or unfaithful, peaceful or not, really *is* somewhere, or whether life just trails off into nothingness like his note's unfinished sentences.

*May our hope remain with us always*, the same monk says in his deep resonating voice, slightly earlier in the service. At least that's how I hear what he says. I'm probably misinterpreting, like a kid getting the words of a popular song wrong. He's almost certainly saying, *May* your help *remain with us always*. But I like to think he's referring to our hope, cautioning us, asking for help for us, to hold onto our hope—through illnesses and hardships, losses and failures, old age, death. Our hope for others, our hope for ourselves. Our hope that life is more than an accident, a tiny space of light between two infinite parentheses of darkness.

A few years back I had a bad night at the monastery. There's one monk who sleeps in the guesthouse and that night my room was next to his and in the middle of the night I was awakened by the soft sound of the monk's door closing. I sat up in bed with a start and was suddenly flooded by fear. At first the fear was nameless, but it quickly took the shape of fear of the monk next door. I imagined how I would feel if I looked over at the doorknob and saw it turning, how I would feel if then the door opened and the monk came into my room. And then I became convinced that that was going to happen at any moment. I got out of bed, tiptoed to the door, and locked it from the inside. Then I got back into bed. But of course I couldn't go back to sleep, and I lay there filled with a nameless terror—a kind of horror, like what you might feel, say, watching the movie *The Exorcist*. I had never experienced anything like that at the monastery before, had always thought of it as a place where you left all your anxieties behind and felt mostly peaceful. I was surprised and abashed to find myself filled with sudden terror there in the middle of the night. But then I remembered my friend Brad, who goes to the monastery a lot, telling me a while back that occasionally he has bad nights there, when he's tormented by ugly thoughts and painful memories and it's extremely unpleasant. And then it came to me, like a thunderclap out of the blue, that I had read something somewhere about very holy places attracting demons as well as angels—that evil spirits are drawn to deeply religious places because they like to try to subvert the goodness there. Now the idea seems silly but at that moment, as I lay on my bed in the monastery, the reality of those demons became an absolute certainty to me—I thought I felt their presence much more strongly than I had ever felt the presence of anything holy there.

I picked up a biography of the famous Trappist monk Thomas Merton, lying on the desk in a pile of books I had borrowed earlier from the monastery library, and started reading it. I knew that Thomas Merton was electrocuted by a fan with a bad connection in Thailand in the 1960s. For some reason I really wanted to find out more about that. I could have easily opened the book at the end and searched until I found the details about the death, but instead I started the book at the beginning and then kept going, skimming some parts, perusing others carefully. I stayed awake all night reading that book.

I learned that Thomas Merton was part of a group of young men at Cambridge University who staged a mock crucifixion and that Merton himself was probably the one who played Christ, that he was almost killed in some accident when they "nailed" him to the cross—Merton himself never publicly confirmed this story but there's evidence to support it. I learned that at the age of fifty-one, when he was a well-known author, priest, and monk at the Abbey of Gethsemani in Kentucky, Merton fell deeply in love with a young student nurse who returned his feelings. They carried on a passionate though celibate affair for several months, Merton sneaking phone calls from the abbey and slipping out for clandestine meetings with S., even rolling around with her in the bushes a few times—until he decided it wasn't right for him to leave the order and gave up the relationship. And I learned, at around five o'clock in the morning, how at the age of fifty-three he gave a speech at a conference in Bangkok, ended it with the words, "so I will disappear from view," then went to his room, took a shower, and was electrocuted by that fan. It was a five-foot-tall floor fan and it fell on top of him, just as the cross might have done during the mock crucifixion years ago in Cambridge, and when they finally got the fan unplugged and off him there was a thick set of burn marks on one side of his dead body.

I lost most of my terror as I was lying on the bed all night, obsessively reading that book till I got to the electrocution at the end, but I never quite lost my sense of the presence of evil, my feeling that there are evil forces at work in the world as well as good ones. I know that Thomas Merton's life was all wrapped up with the good: with reading and writing and prayer and solitary contemplation. But somehow all I could think about was that fan falling on top of him, of the eerie coincidence between his death and his mock crucifixion as a young man at Cambridge, of the horror of Jesus's crucifixion and how that story seemed woven like a dark thread throughout Merton's life.

I used to say that there were demons and angels around Jim Beaman, that I could sense their presence. I loved him for the demons as well as the angels. Those demons ended up taking him, and me, to some horrible places, places I would never want to go to again. Now I'm a little embarrassed about the way I was intrigued by, attracted to, the wildness, self-destructiveness, addictive behavior—those kinds of demons—in him. I could only be attracted to those things when I was naïve enough to think I had the power to change them, naïve enough to think that goodness, hope, love—my love—were strong enough to overcome them, naïve about just how bad things can get. I like to think I could never be that naïve again.

But still, there's something in me that continues to be compelled by the shadowy, not bright-and-sunny parts of life. I never would have stayed up all night reading a book about Thomas Merton if it weren't for the thorny, murky elements of his story. And I'm grateful—at least I think I am—that whoever or whatever made this world created the darkness as well as the light.

"Midway through the journey of our life, I found/myself in a dark wood, for I had strayed/from the straight pathway to this tangled ground." I thought of those lines—the opening of Dante's *Inferno*—the other night when I was lying awake again with insomnia, this time at home in my own bed. I thought of how sometimes when we stray from the straight pathway, wandering or maybe plunging into the brush beside the road, embarking on one of those messy journeys that take us to purgatory and then lower and lower circles of hell, it feels like we've gone somewhere a smarter, wiser, more admirable person would never go. But it came to me in the middle of the night, in a sudden flash of insight, that those journeys are actually the very reason we're here in this world rather than in some other world.

In the weeks and months after Jim Beaman's suicide, I truly thought I would not be able to go on. An endless span of pain and sorrow stretched before me as far as I could see. Every day, every hour seemed like an eternity, and I kept focusing miserably on all the time I was going to have to get through before the end of my life; I figured I probably had twenty-five or thirty years left, maybe twenty if I was lucky.

That was nineteen years ago and I can barely even remember what that felt like. Now, when I look back on that whole thing—the journey that started with me and Beaman on a Sunday morning lying on his rumpled bed and then took him on another day to the same bed, lying there alone with a shotgun pointed at himself, and then took me to a place where I was lying alone in my own bed, smoking cigarettes, trying to wish away all the life I had left—when I look back on all that I see that who I am now is entirely different than who I was then and it was the journey itself, even the very worst moments of it, that made me different. And I don't regret any of it. Of course, it's easy to say that now that I'm past the experience of it. Easy to see how in the moment on Jim Beaman's lawn when the cop told me he was dead and I screamed and screamed, the fingers of the clenched fist with which I had been holding on like a person grabbing wildly onto a branch on the shore, were pried open and I was forced to let go and be swept down the river into life's waiting arms.

# In Jim's Kitchen

I'm swimming around in the deep water of myself when I suddenly find myself in Jim Beaman's kitchen. In the everyday upper air I'm in my friend Anne's living room, it's January 14, 2016, and we're doing EMDR.* It's November 18, 1990 in Jim Beaman's kitchen. He has less than two months to live but we don't know that, of course.

It's a lot better up here in 2016 than it was on that November day in 1990. Anne's living room is spacious and full of light and there are four naughty needy foster kittens in the basement: two orange ones, a dark-gray almost-black one, and one that has silky black-and-white fur that's beautiful enough to be made into a fancy sweater. They were upstairs earlier, nosing around my pocketbook on the hallway floor, climbing Anne's right leg like a tree trunk, nuzzling our necks when we picked them up, and we'll let them come up here again when we're finished and are having our lunch. But we can't have them up here now scratching and climbing and sticking their needy little faces into our faces when we're doing this.

Anne went first this time. While I was sitting there looking through the sliding glass door at her side yard and she was swimming around inside herself—eyes closed, headset on, one alternately-buzzing disk clutched in each hand—I saw the shadow of a tree limb projected onto the trunk of an actual tree in the yard, and then I saw the shadow of a squirrel running across the shadow of the tree limb. Then about a minute later I saw something fly toward the window through my peripheral vision and heard a little bang, the sound of something hitting the glass, and then I thought I saw whatever it was fall to the ground. I was sure it was a bird, and it took all my will power not to get up and go over to that window and look, as if seeing a dead bird lying on the ground could somehow bring it back to life. But I didn't want to freak out Anne, didn't want to give her the bends by calling her back to the surface too quickly or pollute her inner water by throwing something horrible into it from up on the surface, so I didn't say anything, and when Anne was finished with her EMDR and I told her what had happened and we got up and looked out the window, there wasn't any bird there. She said it must've been ice falling out of a tree.

But the feeling of that dead bird wouldn't leave me. It seemed like an appropriate metaphor for the memories and the feelings, the deep dark painful emotional water Anne was traveling around in today, and the water I've been swimming through now, after her, is like that too, poisonous with old unfelt feelings growing out of suppressed memories of deeply painful events. None of which have anything to do with or took place in an era close to the time of that moment in Jim Beaman's kitchen.

But there I am, suddenly, sitting across the table from him. What's this about, I wonder briefly in the EMDR. Is it just a random scrap of memory popping inexplicably into my brain? Or is it some message from my unconscious, here to tell me something about what I'm working on today and if so what?

In the memory I'm making my way through a plate of spaghetti and Italian sausage and Jim is sipping a bottle of beer and watching me eat. It's five o'clock and almost dark, the end of a long gray depressing afternoon; the overhead light shines a queasy yellow florescence onto the table and the dirty pots and pans that fill the sink. I've spent the last forty-five minutes cooking the spaghetti sauce with sausage; it has onions in it too and green peppers. It's not something I would eat now but it was something I made for him and ate with him back then, because he liked it and I liked it well enough too.

I made it on this 1990 late-afternoon because I wanted to do something for him that would help him feel comforted at the end of this long day saturated with depression—his, not mine—and screwed-up brain chemistry resulting from his long night before of sitting at the desk in the bedroom doing, as he would call it, wrong. There's no right left in doing wrong, even for him; it doesn't seem to make him feel even briefly good. But he can't stop doing it and in the aftermath there's this: the sense of failure, the long gray afternoon when the dopamine has receded like water seeping back out of a tidal pool and the dendrites are left dangling in the wind like raw nerve endings. I thought that if I cooked this spaghetti for him and he ate it, it would do a little bit to neutralize all that, that the feeling of being loved and nourished would fill up the hole inside him created by the retreating cocaine. I didn't know it couldn't work that way, and he didn't tell me he wasn't going to be able to eat. Maybe he only figured that out himself once that big steaming plateful of spaghetti was sitting there on the table in front of him.

"Please, go ahead and eat yours," he said apologetically. "It would make me feel better to see you eat it."

So that's what's going on in this window of memory that has opened inside me, a little scrap of 1990 suddenly appearing in the field of 2016. Back in 1990 I still thought I could save him. I still thought he could stop doing wrong if he wanted to or if I said the right convincing thing. I sort of dimly knew we weren't going to have a happy ending but it never once occurred to me it was going to end the way it did. I still thought that love, and I, could put enough goodness into the picture to make it change. I don't know whether Jim still believed that in this moment or whether he had already decided that love hadn't and wasn't going to change anything. I think maybe he did have a pretty good idea, at least more than an inkling, how the story was going to end. But I didn't, and even though I felt deep sympathy for him in this moment, I was also a little bit mad at him because he couldn't or wouldn't stop doing wrong and wouldn't eat what I had cooked for him.

Sometime during the twenty-five years plus a month and a half between now and then, I realized how much sorrow he was feeling himself in that moment. And I came to understand that what was going through his head was not all the stuff about changing-this-so-it-won't-happen-again that was going through mine, but a feeling of being different in some essential way because of his drug problem, of being cut off from real life, of being someone who has to sit by and watch other people eat. That he must've been looking at me as someone who was normal, someone who *could* eat.

But the thing is, that was not who I was back then. It's not even totally who I am now, here in 2016, but it's who I'm trying to become: Someone who can sit at the metaphorical table with other normal people and eat what they eat. I'm groping my way toward becoming that person in this EMDR moment although I don't exactly know that's what I'm doing. I'm getting there by touching down in the places inside me where the I-can't-have-what-other-people-have feeling is, attached to old circumstances and ancient childhood memories that I can barely remember in my current everyday life: living with a foster family, not feeling like I had a mother or a real family or a place in the world. The memories and the circumstances all blend together into one big frozen fog in my inner landscape. I can't really see it and it obscures the view up above in the upper air. But I've been chipping away at it, clearing away bits of it, doing this, with Anne and my therapist Alison at least once a month for years now.

When we're done Anne and I make lunch in her kitchen, throwing salad greens on plates and cutting cherry tomatoes in half and peeling and slicing cucumbers and using a flat white plastic scoop to dish big blobs of rice out of the rice cooker that has been gently percolating on the kitchen counter for the last half hour while we were in the living room, swimming around in the water of our deepest selves. We feel a little woozy and distracted now as we make our lunch, we blink in the light of the bright blaring everyday world which was here all along while we went down to those other worlds, first her, then me. We talk wildly about this and that and laugh about how we can't quite pay attention to what we're doing and saying.

The kittens are back. Anne went to the playroom in the basement and opened the door and now they're racing around the dining room, chasing each other, chasing a little blue ball, skidding across the glossy hard-wood floor, and we stare at them in our dazes and say, over and over, how incredibly, unbelievably cute they are.

And then we sit down opposite each other at the square cherry-wood kitchen table, dish some sliced almonds and sprinkle a little olive oil onto our salads, and eat our lunch.

*EMDR is a kind of psychotherapy that involves healing through dislodging old trapped trauma with the help of bilateral stimulation. The bilateral stimulation can be accomplished in several different ways; we use a small tan flat box and two flat disks and *a headset attached by separate cords to the box. The person who's getting EMDR wears the headset and holds the disks in her hands. The person who's administering the EMDR pushes a button on the box and sits there while the EMDR-ee undergoes twenty or thirty alternating beeps and vibrating buzzes. Anne has the box and we both know how to use it—I've been doing EMDR for years with my regular therapist, and Anne is a therapist—and she and I do EMDR together once a month. Despite its long, uninspired, confusing name—EMDR stands for eye movement desensitization and reprocessing—I find EMDR and the states it takes me to, to be one of the most magical, otherworldly things I've ever been exposed to.*

# Lost and Found

Marek and I are in our bedroom, pulling open drawers and rummaging through them frantically. He has to leave for Chicago at eight a.m. tomorrow so he can fly to the Czech Republic and spend two weeks there and we can't find his passport.

We're in our apartment in the dome house where we live together in Fairfield. Fairfield is a town sixty-five miles south of Iowa City. Maharishi University of Management is there and so are many transcendental meditators. They meditate in twin golden domes, and when Marek started talking about the dome house when we got together—we met when he took a private class I taught in my house—I thought vaguely that he was talking about one of those meditating domes. But it turns out the dome house is a geodesic dome, with high ceilings and octagonal rooms and triangular windows. Marek bought that house in the mid 1990s after his second wife, Barbara, and one of their two little girls, May, died in a car accident on the New Jersey turnpike, and he gave up his life in Boston, sold all his real estate there, and moved to Fairfield, a peaceful place where he could practice transcendental meditation.

He was already remarried by then, to Maria. He and Maria stayed together for eighteen years and had three children. They were beautiful children, and Marek and Maria did their best to bring them up successfully. Marek gave them daddy rides and taught them how to read at very early ages, as he had done with Althea and May.

One of the first things Marek did after moving to Fairfield with Maria and his daughter Althea, the daughter who survived the car accident, was buy the dome house and start fixing it up. He tore out some of the walls in the second-floor apartment and replaced its carpeting and put in a six-foot octagonal skylight at the end of the gallery on the upper floor. He let Althea pick out the colors of the carpet and together they designed a plan for the floor: pink carpet in the living room for fields of strawberries, blue carpet going down the stairs to look like water, green carpet for grass in some other parts of the house. He put stucco on the thirty-foot-high ceiling and then painted it to look like the sky: pinkish clouds on the ceiling in the master bedroom, blue sky with bluish-tinted white clouds in the living room and dining area.

I remember the first time I saw the inside of that house. Marek and Maria were no longer married by then and he and I were living together, but we hadn't been together very long; we were in the first crazy hectic blush of romantic love. Once during that time he knelt before me and tied my shoelace in the grocery store, and every night in bed I read him a piece of *The Rooms of Heaven*, my book about how I lost my fiancé and how I searched for him and then found him in the afterlife and lost myself in the process and then found myself again. Marek and I were in the bedroom in the downstairs apartment in the dome house when we were doing that because there were tenants in the upstairs apartment. We called the downstairs in the dome house Middle Earth because it reminded us of the cozy houses inhabited by hobbits in *The Lord of the Rings*, the movie depictions of which Marek's kids watched over and over at that time. I still had my house in Iowa City then and sometimes we stayed there too. On March 1st the upstairs dome house tenants moved out and nobody else moved in and a couple of days later Marek took me upstairs and showed me that apartment.

I remember standing next to him on the gallery looking down into the empty living room below. The house seemed to me to be full of grief. The acoustics in that place are strange. If you sit in a certain spot in the living room and say something you hear an echo, as if the sound waves travel up to the high ceiling and bounce off and return to you, and it was as if the grief—the old grief of Marek's life, over the death of his beloved wife and daughter, the pain of his older daughter's loss of a mother and sister and even the loss of that daughter herself when she grew up and moved away and finally the loss of his second family, the separation from that wife and the other three kids—it was as if all of that was there and you could feel it, almost hear it along with the silence bouncing and echoing off that strange high ceiling. I remember standing next to Marek feeling all of that, standing there under the ceiling he had painted with a pale blue sky and towering blue-tinted clouds, feeling the magic of the house, the magic of life itself that had brought me to this place with the second great love of my life, who had lost someone like I had and who, completely separate from me, in some track of life parallel to the one I had been traveling, had created the rooms of heaven.

After that I rented my house in Iowa City and Marek and I moved upstairs from Middle Earth into that apartment.

Now I sit in a chair in the living room, get quiet for a few minutes, and ask the universe, my dead boyfriend, St. Anthony, whoever or whatever, to show me where Marek's passport is. I'm confident that if I do this I'll find it. Ever since my fiancé died in 1991, I've been good at finding lost things.

When Jim died I did everything I possibly could to find him—to find his ghost, his spirit, whatever it was that was left of him. Maybe because of the suddenness and violence of his death, the complications of suicide and codependency, I simply could not let him go. I tried to find him by reading books about the afterlife and doing anything else I could. And I have to say that in some ways I did find him, and then I lost him again, and in the process of all that I lost myself and then found myself in a new and more evolved state. Finding myself was very satisfying in a lifelong sort of way but finding him, finding his ghost which I was so desperately searching for, wasn't satisfying even when I seemed to find it. I was always disappointed with whatever I got, and one of the most disappointing things was when some psychic I went to somewhere, said to me, as if passing on a message from my boyfriend's ghost, "He says he can help you find things."

*Really?* I thought. *That's what he can do for me now?*

But ever since then I've had this almost magical ability to find lost things, and the truth is, after my raging desire to find my dead boyfriend died down and then died away forever, that ability to find things has come in very handy.

After I say my little finding prayer I sit quietly for a few more minutes and then I stand up and go to the hallway outside our bedroom. Something makes me open the door of the closet there and for some reason I look on the shelf way on top, above the pole with the coat hangers hanging from it. Underneath a couple of board games and some clothes Marek bought in a thrift store—the games are for his kids although they never play them and the clothes are for Marek's mother, waiting for some day when he will package them up and mail them to her in Prague—I find a pair of khaki pants that belong to Marek. There's a leather belt threaded through the belt loops and in the pocket is an old folded boarding pass and—that's right— Marek's passport. Marek, after kissing and hugging me and saying that he could never get by without me, says that now he remembers leaving the passport in his pocket after going through customs the last time he went back and forth to the Czech Republic.

The next day, after Marek leaves, I realize I haven't seen Madeleine all morning. Madeleine, my fat, anxious, constantly complaining calico cat, the cat I got because my therapist told me to get one because I had an attachment disorder and taking care of a cat would help me heal from that, the cat who was my constant and only companion for years. The fact that I haven't seen her all morning is alarming because she's a compulsive eater and she never misses a meal; always when it's time for feeding she's right there at my feet or in my face, meowing in a way that can't be ignored. I search the house for her and finally I find her lying on her side under a chair. I take her to the vet a couple of hours later, and the vet says she's hurt her back somehow. He tells me to buy a heating pad and put her on it and afterwards I go to Walmart and get one, and although she will have nothing to do with it—she squirms out of my grasp and stalks off when I try to lift her onto it—she starts eating and seems to feel better and I'm enormously relieved.

I'm driving to Fairfield from Iowa City in my little red Honda. There are rolling cornfields all the way to the horizon on both sides of the car and I can see them in the rearview mirror too. The empty road unfurls behind me in the mirror and stretches out ahead beyond the windshield, nothing but a narrow gray two-lane road bisecting the vast cornfields, ditches and weeds at the edge of the road, blackbirds sitting on telephone wires, the blue sky overhead piled high with towering cumulus clouds. Ordinarily I love this view—I've lived in Iowa for almost twenty years now and I still feel lucky to be in a place where there's so much nothing you can see the horizon—but today I'm driving through it full of heel-dragging dread. I'm not noticing much of anything and what I do see doesn't give me any pleasure.

I've spent the weekend in Iowa City and now I'm going home—home with quotation marks around it. I live in the dome house in Fairfield, it's true, but it doesn't feel like home and I don't want to go there. But I have to. There's something deeply familiar about the feeling I'm having in this moment, deeply familiar about this whole situation, and it's stunning to me the way that Life with a capital L has managed to recreate the conditions and emotions of my childhood so incredibly accurately: A mother who hates me (an ex-wife in this case); a father I love (this time a boyfriend) who needs me to live with him, exposing me to the rage of the mother (ex-wife); the longing to stay in the place where I feel safe (the Paysons' house in my childhood, Iowa City now); the heel-dragging dread, the sinking in the pit of my stomach, the sense of going toward something that I *really, really* do not want to go to, mingled with the guilt about not wanting to go there, the conflicted feelings around the man. How is it possible that all these coincidences, this confluence of similarities, can be happening? It's as if there's something purposeful about life itself, I think, not for the first time, with life somehow miraculously crafting stories that replicate your earlier life and comment on your psychology.

There's a red Ford Explorer parked in the driveway when I arrive at the dome house. The dome house, sheltered under oak and olive trees, with its low rounded shake-shingled roof, looks like a big mushroom or a hobbit house or something out of a fairy tale, and I feel like someone out of a fairy tale when I see the red vehicle sitting in the driveway: Snow White or Gretel or one of those other fairy tale girls threatened by witches or step mothers—those women who want to feed you poison apples, cook you in the oven, track you down where you're hiding among the dwarves in the woods. In this case she is Marek's ex-wife and in the past she was my mother and it's as if the two of them have merged in this moment—they're merging in my unconscious; their hate feels exactly the same to me, it has exactly the same quality and coloration and feeling tone, but maybe that's because they're playing on the same piano key inside me.

Maria hates me in the same way my mother did and for the same reasons, except that my mother hated me because I wouldn't live at home and Maria hates me because I do, because I live in this house with Marek. It's easy to see why Maria, still fresh from the divorce and not yet ready to let go of the illusion that he and she are going to get back together, hates me for that. Hates me for being there in the house with him, an inconvenient presence getting in the way of their reconciliation, though Marek keeps insisting that they're not going to get back together no matter what.

It's less obvious why my mother hated me for living with another family. When I was a kid I had no idea at all why my mother hated me for living with the Paysons, why she hated them so much we had to pretend they didn't exist when we were around her. It was just something I took for granted, just a condition of my life like not wanting to go to school or hating winter, and it's taken me years to come to understand it at all. To understand and even sympathize with how threatening and upsetting, even life-ruining, it would be to have a child who's so afraid of you she keeps running away from you, a child who insists on living with somebody else instead of with *you*.

I pull into the dome-house driveway and park next to the red Explorer. I open my car door and get out just as the house's front door opens and the two kids emerge—they're twelve and nine, strong, smart, beautiful, normal children who do their best to juggle the child-needs of the adults around them—and behind them is Maria. I glance at her—I see long wavy auburn hair, a frowning face—and quickly look away, my heart pounding, breath coming shallowly, knees going weak with fear at the mere sight of her, at the knowledge that she can see *me* there in the driveway, her nemesis, the cause of all her problems and her pain.

Marek stands on the raised front deck looking down as Maria and the kids get into the van, Maria frowning angrily as she opens the driver's side door, the kids looking dutiful, self-conscious, vaguely guilty as they open their doors and climb in, one onto the front seat and one into the back, their eyes carefully averted from me the whole time. Marek comes down and stands next to me and I go limp with relief as Maria pulls out of the driveway and the car disappears down the street. But then Marek says to me, "Somebody let Madeleine out last night. The kids and I tried to find her but we couldn't. She's a cat—she probably hasn't gone very far away."

I turn to Marek and say, "I knew I shouldn't have brought her down here to Fairfield," and then I burst out bawling in a loud hysterical way that surprises even me. Marek puts his arms around me and pulls me to his chest. Later he will say he was shocked by the violence of my emotion in that moment, and I won't even try to explain to him that I was crying because Madeleine was lost but also because I was lost, that I had lost myself, was losing myself, in *him*—by living in his house, his town, his life instead of in my own. That Madeleine was all I had left of my old life, the life I had lived in my own house with only her for years, and if she was gone that life and myself in it were truly gone too. And not only that, but Madeleine, with her kitty sadness and insecurity, her defenselessness and in-nocence, was kind of like a symbol, a real-world dream symbol somehow magically produced by my particular psychology, of the sad, innocent, insecure part of me: the child part who was afraid of my mother and was afraid of Maria now. That little girl had always been lost and now she was out there roaming around the streets in the form of my cat Madeleine with no way to get home and no hope of getting home and no one to rescue her but me. I won't say all that to Marek when we talk later about my overwhelming reaction to her being lost, because I don't know how and because I'm afraid it'll hurt his feelings and besides, I only dimly know it myself.

I spent what was left of the day walking around the neighborhood calling *Madeleine! Madeleine!* over and over. I walked on streets I'd never been on before, past houses where people I didn't know were having ordinary late Sunday afternoons and early evenings; the people in those houses seemed alien to me and so did the town and the neighborhood. I knew I'd never find Madeleine on those streets, but I couldn't stop looking for her, calling her name hopelessly, ranging farther and farther from the dome house. I truly felt that if I couldn't find her I would not be able to go on—not knowing where she was, all the time feeling that she was out there wandering around lost, confused, terrified—but as the hours passed and night got closer I started thinking that the chances of finding her were getting dim, that if I didn't find her that day I probably never would.

Finally, at about seven-thirty, when the light was starting to fade, I went home and called my only friend in Fairfield, Ellen John, because she'd told me she was a little bit psychic and I wanted to hear what she would say about where Madeleine was, and also because I needed a friend in that moment, needed to talk someone friendly in Fairfield who wasn't Marek. Ellen said she had the feeling Madeleine was somewhere behind the house.

I went out behind the dome house and stood beside a big hydrangea bush, facing a sagging chicken wire fence at the edge of Marek's property, and called and called— *Maaaadeleine! Maaaadeleine!* I called that name so many times I got into a kind of trance where I lost track of time and even for a moment of what I was doing. And then, like a little miracle, I heard a squeaky nervous tentative *meow*, and there she was sticking her white head out the top of the big bush beside me. I rushed inside and got a can of cat food, opened it and put it down on the grass, and when she crouched over it I scooped her up and carried her through the back door into the house.

I can honestly say that was one of the happiest moments of my life.

# Marigold

I'm in my car outside the jail in Ottumwa, Iowa. Marek's inside, visiting our friend and roofer, Phil, who's in jail for discharging a firearm within city limits. It's a little more complicated than that too, Phil's not supposed to have a firearm at all because he has some sort of minor criminal record or something. So he's stuck in here for a month and Marek wanted to visit him to try to raise his spirits. I'm sitting out here waiting for Marek. I don't want to go inside the jail. The reason I'm here is that I'm Marek's driver, now and for the next two months.

I don't mind driving Marek around for the most part, taking him on his errands and to his appointments. Sometimes he reads me the poems in the New Yorker, and we talk about his childhood in Prague and mine outside of Northampton, and we look at the wide blue ever-changing Iowa sky, full of towering cumulus clouds that turn orange and pink and then deep purple as the light fades and evening comes on, and describe it to each other. Marek likes these moments too. Years later, when I'm no longer driving him around and there's another woman in the car with him, Marek will remember being ferried around the Iowa countryside by me—reading poetry, describing the sky—so fondly it will make him cry.

But right now, in this moment, he can't stand not being able to drive himself, not so much the not-driving but the reason behind it. If you get three traffic tickets in a year in the state of Iowa you lose your license for a couple of months. That's what happened to Marek, to his outrage and dismay—Marek hates the state, not the state as in the state of Iowa but the state as in the government, the bureaucracy, that threatening Big Brotherly machine which was Communism back when he was living in Czechoslovakia and now lives on inside his head. The state came down on Phil after he fired that gun just for fun, one afternoon in his yard because he was drunk, and it's coming down on Marek by taking his license away. So here I am, waiting outside the jail in Ottumwa.

It's September, about four-thirty in the afternoon, and it's pleasantly warm and bright in the car. Spot, our little black-and-white mutt, is sitting in the passenger seat beside me and I don't mind being here at all. Then in the rearview mirror I see Marek emerging from the jail, walking across the parking lot.

"Did you see?" he says as soon as he gets the door open. "There's a kitten over there. She meows at whoever goes in and comes out. I didn't see her when I went in."

"Oh!" I say. "Let's go look."

I get out of the car and Marek and I cross the parking lot. As we approach the jail someone comes out and a tiny brownish-gray kitten standing on some gravel to the left of the door meows at him in a loud plaintive voice. The guy doesn't even glance down at her.

"Oh my gosh," I say.

Marek bends down and pets the kitten and I bend down and pick her up.

"What should we do?" I say. "We can't just leave her here."

"I don't really want to have another cat," Marek says. "One cat is enough."

"I don't really want to have another cat either," I say, thinking of my cat Madeleine and how much she'd hate having a little rival in the house.

There's a pause.

"Well, we can't just leave her here," Marek says.

We go inside the building, me holding the kitten against my shoulder. She stays perfectly still, doesn't squirm to get down the way most kittens would.

"Does this cat belong to anyone?" I ask the burly policeman seated behind the front desk.

"Not that I know of," he says. "She's been out there for a while."

"Is it okay if we take her with us then?" I ask.

The policeman grins and nods vigorously.

And that's how we come by the newest member of our family.

When we open the doors to get in the car Spot jumps into the back and Marek sits in the passenger seat, holding the kitten on his lap. I get in behind the wheel and start the car and the kitten looks up at me, a wide-eyed inquiring look on her face. She climbs onto Marek's shoulder, sees Spot on the backseat, arches her back, and hisses a tiny kitten hiss.

"Ouch!" Marek says. "She stuck her claws in me." He disengages her from his shirt and puts her on the floor by his feet.

On the way home we discuss what to do with her. At first we think we're going to bring her to the animal rescue place and all we're doing is getting her off the street, but by the time we get home we've decided to let her live with us but stay outside and be an outdoor cat.

I like the idea of letting the new kitten be an outdoor cat. I'm worried that Madeleine will beat her up and injure her and I'm also worried that Madeleine will feel jealous and upset. Keeping the kitten outside appeals to Marek too. He isn't crazy about Madeleine, doesn't want to let her in our bedroom or let her sleep on the bed with us but it's impossible to keep her out or off—if we close the bedroom door with her on the outside she meows in a loud voice impossible to ignore and puts her paw under the door and bangs it back and forth, and once she's in the room we can't keep her off the bed. I already feel guilty enough about all the fuss caused by Madeleine and I feel guilty on Madeleine's behalf too because I uprooted her last spring to move here and live with Marek, and I'm thinking that leaving this kitten outside is a way to avoid further guilt.

It's getting dark and it's a little cold by the time we get to the house. I carry the kitten up the stairs of the deck and put her down, go inside and get some of Madeleine's canned food and a bowl while Marek waits outside with her. Back on the deck I put a tablespoon of the food into the bowl and the kitten eats it ravenously and I give her some more. Marek takes a square thin plastic cushion off a deck chair and bends it into a triangle and puts it under the chair. I pick up the kitten and put her inside the small house of the cushion and say to her, "See? It's a little chalet."

The kitten sits in there for a few minutes, staring out at me with what I swear is a look of dread and dismay—"No one but you thinks there are expressions on cats' faces," Marek will tell me on another occasion—and then she sticks out her front legs, pulls herself up and out of her little house, and stands at our feet gazing up at us. It's getting darker and colder by the moment and I think of coyotes and owls that capture small animals and run into the woods or flap their big wings and carry them off into the night and I say to Marek, "I'm not leaving her out here."

Marek doesn't protest and we take her into the house. I carry her directly upstairs to my study before Madeleine can even get a look at her and I leave her in there with some more food and water and one of Madeleine's cat boxes.

There's something scaly and strange-looking on her tail— Marek says she has a tail-eating disease—and when I take her to the vet the next day the vet says she has a broken tail. Then he reaches out and removes about three inches from the end of it. I'm horrified but the kitten doesn't even seem to notice. The vet also says she's malnourished and probably would have starved to death in a few days if we hadn't rescued her. He wraps a bandage around the end of her tail, saying that the tip, where you can see a little bit of white bone showing through the fur, will heal. If it doesn't, he says, he'll fix it in a couple of weeks. I take her home and bring her back to my study, where she lies on the daybed and sleeps for almost a week, waking up with a little chirrup, rising to my hand to be petted, whenever I come into the room.

Her tail doesn't heal, and I have to take her back to the vet three more times. The last time we go, the vet holds her down on the table, pulls two little flaps of tail fur over the white bone tip and stitches the ends of the fur together, and the kitten, whom Marek's daughter and I have named Marigold, squirms and struggles mightily under the doctor's hand and finally lets out a long tortured yowl, the scream of some untamed creature caught in a trap, a wild animal much bigger, fiercer, and more despairing than one would ever imagine a kitten could be.

She will grow up to be a small cat with a short pointy-ended tail, unnaturally soft fur, one peach-colored paw, and large intelligent green eyes. She hops onto my lap every morning and sits there while I meditate for twenty minutes, sometimes looking up into my face and giving me one of her long searching gazes.

She's a quiet peaceful presence in my house, but she will always be afraid to go the doctor. The minute she catches sight of me carrying the pet taxi up the basement stairs she disappears and hides for at least a day. And I know, because I heard that scream in the Fairfield vet's office, because we found her lost outside, wandering around in the world, and because sometimes in the spring she stands at the back door and cries loudly, longingly, to be let out to roam around and get lost again, that she harbors some deep atavistic sorrow, and in her heart she's still a wild creature, feral and untamed.

# Eek

The first one looked like a brown blob on my hallway floor—it was one o'clock in the morning and I didn't have my contact lenses in. I'd gotten up to go to the bathroom and I might have just gone back to bed if it hadn't been for the excited way my cat Meme—Meme is Madeleine's successor—was crouching beside the blob, staring at it totally transfixed. It looked limp, wet, boneless, and I was sure it was dead, then Meme pounced on it and it squeaked and hopped—weakly, as if marshaling its last bit of energy to get away—to a spot near the bottom of the stairs. Meme followed it and pounced on it again. I was instantly transported into a state of terror, as if I'd just discovered a murderer or some other dangerous intruder in my house instead of a little brown, defenseless, half-dead mouse.

I had no idea what to do about it but I knew I had to do something. I went into my bedroom and put on my shoes. By the time I got back it had found its way to the metal cold-air-return grill set in the hallway floor. I picked up the entire narrow, foot-and-a-half-long grill and carried it to the back-door, opened the door and shook the mouse off onto the step. I slammed the door and stood there shaking.

"The only thing we have to fear is fear itself," FDR famously said, and I've never before so clearly felt the truth of that statement. In a strange way the mouse's fear was almost as distressing as my own. It's as if the mouse's fear *was* my fear, as if the mouse and I were one, united in our fear of each other, in our fear of. . . whatever. Standing there in my kitchen in the middle of the night in a t-shirt, underpants, and tennis shoes, I congratulated myself on facing my fear, on saving the mouse from my cat, and most of all on getting rid of the mouse. The worst thing, I thought, would be knowing it was somewhere in the house and not knowing where or how to get it out.

My cat looked at me reproachfully, as if I'd stolen her toy.

At that point I still thought having a mouse was going to be a one-time-only occurrence—I'd never had a mouse in this house before. So I was surprised, shocked, and more than a little dismayed when, just as I was drifting off to sleep the following night, I heard banging in the kitchen, got up, and went in there to find both cats—Meme and Marigold—pursuing a little brown thing around the splayed-foot pedestal at the base of the table. It squeaked as Meme crouched, chased it half a foot across the floor, and grabbed it with her mouth. It dangled there for a minute before she dropped it, then Marigold got hold of it and it dangled from her mouth, she dropped it and it ran behind the kitchen table leg, Meme reached out a paw and batted it. I snatched up the plastic bowl of my salad spinner, which was sitting on my kitchen counter, hoping to capture the mouse in that, but before I could get near it it ran under the oven. Both cats settled down next to the stove, avidly eyeing the space at the bottom. I went back to bed but couldn't go back to sleep for several hours.

The next night I went to bed early, exhausted from my previous night's mouse-in-the-kitchen insomnia, and was awakened from a deep satisfying sleep at about one in the morning by Meme pouncing on the blankets covering my legs. I heard squeaking, opened my eyes and saw something small and brown running up the quilt toward my head. Meme was crouching, getting ready to pounce again. Before I could think about what I was doing or was even fully awake I jumped out of bed, grabbed Meme and stuck her in my study—I had to shove her back in a few times before I successfully closed the door in her face—then I ran into the kitchen and got the bowl and the top of the salad spinner, which were once again conveniently sitting on the counter.

Back in the bedroom the mouse was nowhere to be seen. I lifted a flap in the bedclothes and there was it, hiding in a little tunnel made by the fold. I placed the salad spinner bowl on top of it, lifted the bowl and quickly turned it over so the mouse fell to the bottom and I could clap the salad spinner top on. I took it to my back door, opened the door and stepped outside—barefoot and wearing only some underpants and a t-shirt—removed the top from the salad spinner and dumped the mouse onto the grass beside the step. I went back in the kitchen and closed the door behind me, still just barely awake but feeling vastly relieved. At that point I was still thinking all I had to do was put the mouse outside, and I was still thinking that each mouse would be the last mouse, the only mouse after just a couple of other mice. It never occurred to me that there could be more or that some of them, as someone told me later, could be the same mouse coming back in.

When I opened the door to my study Meme rushed out and ran into the bedroom. She jumped onto the bed and began carefully sniffing every spot on the covers where the mouse must've been. I knew I should get up and launder all the bed clothes but I didn't have the energy, especially since my antique Amish quilt can only be washed by hand in the bathtub. So instead I got into bed and tried to forget about what had been touching the covers just a few minutes earlier, a task that was made more difficult by the way Meme continued to sniff deeply, with a rapt, thoughtful, slightly distressed expression on her face, various spots on the quilt.

Having gone from being deeply asleep to thoroughly awake in a few seconds, and having experienced a tremendous jolt of adrenaline a few seconds after waking, I couldn't go back to sleep. I had jumped out of bed and taken action without really thinking about it, but as I lay there in bed I replayed what had happened over and over, feeling about as creeped-out as it's possible to feel. I kept reliving the moment when I opened my eyes and saw the mouse and the adrenaline jolt struck, kept imagining how I would feel if another mouse showed up, transported onto the bed by Meme, and woke me up. Strangely, it didn't occur to me to get up and close the bedroom door to keep Meme out. I just lay awake in bed for hours—one hour, two hours, three hours, four hours—not sleeping, not even relaxing, jolting awake in a kind of re-enactment of my original adrenaline rush whenever I started to drift off. I was miserable and exhausted the next day.

I happened to have a pre-existing psychotherapy appointment the day after that. I told my therapist about my nocturnal visit by a mouse and she said right away, "Let's do EMDR on it."

She got out her bi-lateral stimulation gadget, untangled the wires and plugged them into the small tan box, and handed me the headphones and disks. I put the headphones on and grasped one disk in each hand; she pushed a button on the little box and I sank down inside myself while the beeps sounded quietly and the disks vibrated gently, back and forth, back and forth, on alternating sides, and I relived that moment when I woke up with a mouse on my bed.

I traveled back to the fear, just as I've been doing every couple of weeks for longer than I care to say, trying to track down other kinds of fear: old fear, hidden fear, mostly fear of my mother, who, I've figured out with the help of Alison, had postpartum mental illness and probably borderline personality disorder. The fear of my mother is much more complex and has been much harder to track down and corner in the airy insubstantial world of my unconscious than the fear of the mouse, except for in the way that the fear of the mouse *was* the fear of my mother, since all fear springs from the same place and all fears seem to mingle together in that place, to merge and overlap and become one another.

The EMDR on the mouse seemed to help. When one turned up in my kitchen in the middle of the night about a week after my therapy session, I noticed that I wasn't quite so scared.


For something that's cute, small, harmless, and innocent, mice have a very bad reputation. "They're sneaky," Marek's son Val said in an unfriendly blame-the-mouse tone of voice, as if mice are doing something underhanded by trying to avoid being caught in traps or tortured by cats.

"They spread disease!" my friend Honor said, with more than a tinge of hysteria. "If I were you I'd call an exterminator. And I certainly hope you're not using that salad spinner for anything but catching mice now!"

"Why can't you just catch them and kill them like everybody else?" my boyfriend Marek said grumpily.

"Isn't Meme doing a good thing by catching them?" my friend Susan asked me kindly.

"I suppose," I said.

I couldn't seem to make anyone understand, maybe didn't want to make them understand, that I felt *sorry* for the mice. I felt horrified by their terror of the cats and by their suffering in the hands—in the paws and claws and teeth—of the cats. And even though I knew, of course, that it's idiotic, irrational, and anthropomorphizing to feel pity for vermin, and even though I wanted the mice out of my house more than anything, I didn't want to kill them, and I felt troubled and deeply sorrowful when something or someone did. I still feel obscurely proud that out of seventeen mice that came into my house that fall, only three died: One drowned in the dog's water bowl, one expired in the snow after I transported it to a snow bank at the end of the street, and one—but only one—was tortured to death by the cats; Marek found it on the kitchen table in the morning, neatly placed on the spot where my plate goes during meals. He said it was still breathing a little so he didn't flush it down the toilet—down the toilet!—instead he picked it up by the tail and put it beside a bush outside my back door. I found it there later, its eyes squeezed shut and its pinched face set in a little open-mouthed death mask.

I managed to rescue all the other mice. I got better at it as I went along. I became proficient at clapping the salad spinner bowl over one of those little gray or tan creatures, even while it was running, and I learned how to neatly turn the bowl and clap on the top before the mouse could scoot out. I figured out that I had to take the mice all the way to the end of my dead-end street and release them in a spot at the edge of the woods looking down on the railroad tracks, to eliminate the possibility of the mouse turning around and coming back into my house (although I can't imagine what mouse would be stupid enough to risk being mauled *again* by two cats). I learned that mice loathe the smell of peppermint ("it's like dog shit to us," someone explained) and that putting a couple of drops of peppermint oil on a couple of cotton balls and placing the cotton balls around your house worked like a charm in keeping mice away in some people's houses although not mine.

It became almost routine to get up in the middle of the night and rescue some mouse. I even got to the point where I could fairly calmly chase down a running cat with a mouse dangling from its mouth, pick up the cat and hold it over the salad spinner bowl and shake it until it let go of the mouse. I learned, with the help of EMDR and a lot of practice, that mice really aren't that scary, and then I learned something I would never have dreamed of when I saw that first nearly dead brown blob on my floor, which is that some mice are scarier than others.

Mice *sing*. Not long ago researchers discovered that mice squeak in regular, repeating patterns, the way birds tweet. Researchers identified a number of different song patterns shared by a variety of mice and learned that individual mice have their own unique songs which they repeat over and over during the course of a lifetime.

I kept thinking of that during my prolonged mouse siege. Even though I got sort of used to having a mouse show up some nights in my kitchen, and even though I wasn't nearly as scared of the mice as I had been in the beginning, the mice wore me down. I felt nervous inside my house in a way I hadn't before, and after a while I started imagining mice when there were none. Sometimes at night in my bedroom I'd hear the cats making noise in the kitchen and I'd run in there, sure I'd find a mouse being pursued under the table, but there would be no mouse. And occasionally I imagined I heard squeaking and wondered if it could be the sound of a mouse singing. But then I'd think that whatever squeaking there was in my cat-inhabited house probably wasn't singing but more like screaming.

The mice stopped coming into my house when it got really cold and I thought my siege was over. Then one warm sunny Saturday afternoon at the beginning of March, I was lying on the daybed in my study reading a novel with Marigold curled up beside my legs, when I heard Meme pouncing, banging, chasing in fits and starts in the kitchen and I heard—this time I definitely heard it—one loud, frightened mouse squeak.

Marigold jumped down from the bed and raced purposefully into the kitchen and I followed her. I grabbed the salad spinner out of the cabinet, waited for Meme to drop the mouse, and placed the plastic bowl on top of it. It was, I saw, after I had turned over the bowl, clapped on the top, and had a chance to peer through the plastic at my new little captive, a very small mole-gray mouse. Its fur was wet from being in Meme's mouth, and it was shaking like a leaf as if it had been thoroughly traumatized by its encounter with life in my kitchen. It continued to tremble as I carried it down the street in its see-through prison; its legs were bare and pink. I dumped it on a pile of leaves at the edge of the woods and it stayed there without moving, and then it slowly walked a couple of inches forward and disappeared into a hole in the ground I hadn't noticed before. There was something about that particular mouse—maybe its terrified shaking, the fact that it appeared to be a baby, an innocent suddenly confronted by the unexpected horrors of the world—that made me sad whenever I thought about it, and I kept worrying in the days that followed—yes, I admit it, I was worrying about a mouse—about that hole it crawled into and what might've happened to it once it got in there.

One thing that became apparent to me during my long mouse siege was my tendency toward denial: I kept thinking that each and every mouse would be the last mouse, no matter how much evidence there was to the contrary. With every mouse, there would be the initial shock of recognition—yes, eek, that's a mouse running across the floor, that's a live rodent dangling from my cat's mouth—then there would be the marshaling of energy to do something about it, the fear that this time I wouldn't be able to get rid of it, the stress and distaste while getting rid of it, and then the relief—whew!—afterwards, walking back along the sidewalk with a light step and an easy heart, carrying the empty salad spinner. The mouse was gone, it hadn't died or suffered overly much, and now I could return to my house knowing I was alone in it again. I cycled through those feelings with every single mouse. I was sure that every mouse was going to be the last mouse.

And so I was shocked once again when another small mouse showed up in my kitchen the day after I got rid of the gray one who went down the hole. This mouse too appeared to be a baby; it didn't run very far or fast to try to get away from the cats, when Meme dropped it at one point it landed on its back and waved its little legs comically in the air. It was light tan and easy to catch, and although it still appeared to be alive when I dropped it off in the leaves at the end of the street, it didn't move. It seemed doubtful that it would survive, and I comforted myself by imagining it being joined by the little gray baby mouse who had somehow miraculously made his way back out of that hole.

The day after that I had lunch with my friend Anne and her seven-year-old son Paul, and afterwards they waited in their car in my driveway while I went inside to retrieve a book I had borrowed from Anne. As soon as I arrived in my kitchen I saw that both cats were displaying their typical riveted mouse-alert behavior and sure enough, there on the floor between them was a little brown mouse. I slapped the salad spinner bowl, dome-like, over it, got Anne's book and quickly brought it out to her in her car in the driveway, told her what was going on, and then ran back into the house to deal with the mouse. A few minutes later Anne and Paul came to my back door. "Paul wants to see the mouse," Anne said.

I held the salad spinner up to show its contents to Paul. Then they walked down to the end of the street with me and watched while I dumped the mouse out onto the ground. Paul was worried that it would make its way to the railroad tracks down at the bottom of the long wooded embankment and get run over by a train.

"Don't worry, honey," Anne said, "it won't go all the way down there."

"I think that's the least of its problems," I said.

After we had stared at the little mouse for a while—it didn't run away like some of them did but instead just stood shivering in the leaves—we walked back to my house, and on the way Anne said to me, "I hate to tell you this, but that mouse was born in your house."

I paused for a minute to let the meaning of that sink in. Anne and Paul got into their car and drove off and I went back into my house with a new level, or maybe a renewed level, of mouse anxiety.

"The nest is probably somewhere in the kitchen," Marek said when I told him on the phone what Anne had said. "They like to be warm and near the food source." As strange as it may seem, that was a relief to me—I had been picturing the mouse nest in the basement, impossible to find among Marek's stored junk, my tools and half-empty bottles of cleaning supplies, the wires and cement blocks and exposed tufts of insulation.

Marek and I were carrying on a long-distance relationship by then; he was still living in Fairfield and I was back in my house in Iowa City. "Can you come this afternoon and help me find it?" I asked him.

He showed up at four. His twenty-one-year-old son Val, who was living near me in Iowa City, came too, not to help us find the nest but to help Marek load some stuff onto a trailer and join us for dinner. Val was outside cleaning out my shed while Marek searched for the mouse nest in my kitchen: pulled out the stove and looked behind it, pulled the cabinet that holds the microwave away from the wall, looked behind another cabinet—nothing. And then it came to me where the mama mouse must be. In my kitchen beside the stove is long door about the width of an ironing board; it looks like there might've been an ironing board behind it at some time but now there are shallow shelves; at one point I put some vitamins and spices there and then forgot about them.

Marek opened the door and said, in a hushed voice, "There she is." Crouched on the shelf, her eyes big and black, was a very large mouse, a mouse that you knew immediately was a mother mouse dedicated to keeping her babies safe, if any of those babies were still around instead of out in the cold at the end of my street, being eaten by who knows what in non-mouse holes or carried away by owls or starving to death in the leaves. It was shocking to me, somehow, to see that mother mouse crouching on that shelf, perfectly still, staring straight ahead through large dark frightened eyes, as if she was hoping to be invisible.

"Capture her in this!" I said to Marek, handing him the salad spinner.

But before he could even get near her she had gotten away. He didn't see where she went and neither did I. I felt annoyed by our or, to tell you the truth, his, bumbling incompetence, and he got annoyed at my annoyance and we had a little fight, standing there in the kitchen among the stove and the cabinets pulled out halfway across the floor. Of course, I was irritated by the fact that we had come so close to capturing the mama mouse and now she was still in my house, on her way to building more nests, having more babies, and eventually I apologized to Marek and we both got over it. We pushed the stove and cabinets back, I washed the shelves in the ironing-board closet with soap and bleach, we made dinner, called in Val, and sat down to eat.

We had just finished and were still sitting at the table talking when Meme, who had been nosing around in a spot where we leave our shoes by the back door, suddenly pounced, snatched the mama mouse from her hiding place, and sprinted toward the living room, the mouse held sideways in her mouth like a little football.  Marek, Val, and I stood up, I grabbed the salad spinner, and all three of us—two big tall men and a middle-aged woman—chased after my cute fuzzy black-and-white cat, who had learned from her previous encounters with mice and me that when she got hold of one she had to outrun me.  She raced into the living room, her fat little determined-looking butt well ahead of us the whole way.

"It's on the couch!" Marek said.  I ran toward the couch with my salad spinner but by that time the mama mouse had disappeared.

"She's fast," Val said.

"*Shit*," I said.

I glanced down and saw something on the floor.  Marek leaned over, picked it up, and held it out:  It was a tiny dead baby mouse, the size of a baby's little finger, its closed eyes slits, its crabbed feet like miniature monkey paws. "How did *that* get here?" I said.  I pictured the baby mouse clinging to its mother's bosom, dying of fright during its mother's frantic trip through the living room, being flung off by centrifugal force.  Or worse, the baby dying earlier and the mother carrying its corpse around with her.  Marek tossed the tiny dead body into the trash in the kitchen, then came back and pulled out the couch, and we looked along the floorboards behind it for the mother.

"I don't see it," Val said, and because there was nothing left to do in the living room he drifted back to the kitchen.

"I hope she didn't go down the heating vent into the basement," I said to Marek.

"I think she did," Marek said.  I reached over and belatedly closed the vent.

That night Marek and Val finished loading stuff onto

Marek's trailer, Val left for his apartment in Iowa City, and Marek drove back to Fairfield. I was left in my house alone. Except that I wasn't alone.

I had gotten sort of used to the other mice, but that mother mouse totally freaked me out. Marek kept going on about her, before he left that night and then when we talked on the phone the next day—he had gotten the best look at her, in that moment when he opened the ironing-board cabinet door before she raced away—and he kept saying she had three colors in her fur, like a calico cat. He also kept talking about how big and fast she was, how she could run up walls, squeeze through tiny spaces, hide in all sorts of places, as if she was some kind of mouse super power.

In the days that followed I saw nothing more of her. Before, when there was some mouse in the house that had gotten away and was hiding under the stove or the piano, I had felt uncomfortably *not alone*. But now I experienced the not-alone feeling on a much deeper level. It was as if something truly terrifying was hiding in my house, something that might jump out at me at any moment, bringing to the surface all the fear I had ever felt in my life. I knew, of course, that the mama mouse wouldn't jump out—she was hiding and would continue hiding, but somehow that only made things worse. And I also knew, of course, that the whole scary phenomenon, every bit of it, was in my imagination. But that didn't help at all.

In my imagination the mama mouse wasn't tiny, meek, and vulnerable as the other mice had been, and I didn't feel sorry for her the way I had for them—it was only squeamishness that kept me from wanting to squish, snap, or poison her. It was her mother-ness, I guess, that really scared me, her largeness, her authority, her ability to reproduce. Her huge weird watchful mournful eyes. It seems safe to assume that my fear of the mouse was somehow rooted in my fear of my mother, but I wasn't consciously aware of that. The mouse, or rather the mouse's qualities, didn't remind me of my mother—my mother wasn't particularly protective or watchful. And I'm not afraid of mothers in general. But still. I didn't like thinking of a mouse being a mother. Of an almost larger-than-life mouse having almost human qualities.

And then, as happens so often with fear, after a few days I kind of got used to the idea of having her in the house, I thought maybe she had found some way out, I thought maybe the whole thing would just go away.

"Look what was in my apartment in Fairfield," Marek said the next time he came to visit. "A mouse trap!" He held out a square tin trap with the words Ketch All printed on a piece of paper stuck to the side. The next day, after he left, I smeared some peanut butter in one of its two holes, turned the key to activate the mechanism, and set the trap on the floor beside a cabinet in the kitchen. A week went by and nothing happened, and I continued to hope that the mama mouse had somehow magically gone away. Then one early evening I noticed Marigold nosing around the Ketch All. I carried the trap outside. It was light and I was pretty sure it was empty so I didn't even bother taking it all the way to the end of the street. I just went down about four houses, set the trap on the ground under a tree, and lifted the trap's little metal door. I thought I saw a large frantic mouse shoot out, race across a lawn, and disappear into the twilight.

After that my mouse siege came to an end. It's been at least four years since a mouse has appeared in my kitchen and I've stopped expecting one to show up at any minute, though every now and then, when my cats are racing around the house in the middle of the night, engaging in one of those fits of feline madness all cats are regularly overtaken by, I lie in bed worrying that if I get up and go out to the kitchen I'll find them torturing a little brown or gray intruder. But I never do get up, and the cats always calm down after ten or fifteen minutes and in the morning I find them lying around on the daybed or perching casually on the back of the couch and I feel reassured that my house is still mouse-less.

For a long time I continued to believe that the mother mouse had exited the Ketch All trap the night I took it down the street and opened it under a tree by my neighbor's house. Then two falls ago, when I had my furnace inspected, the heating and air conditioning guy paused in my kitchen on his way out to his truck to get a new filter. "Look what I found in your furnace," he said, holding up a flat dead mouse by its tail. It looked a little bigger than an ordinary mouse, its greasy fur was mottled, and I immediately knew it was the mother mouse.

She hadn't disappeared into the dusk and escaped to freedom, the night I brought the Ketch All down the street and opened the door to release whatever was in there. Instead she'd taken the only escape route available to her when Marek, Val, and I were chasing her, squeezing through an iron vent and plunging down a slippery chute to a certain death in a dark sealed-off place. For the briefest instant I felt her terror, her panic at being pursued by a cat and three human beings, her sorrow over the dead baby and the children who had been carried to the end of the street and dumped into the leaves. I felt strangely shocked by that vision, or maybe what shocked me was the sight of her dangling ignominiously by her tail from the grinning repairman's callused fingers, the realization that even those we're the most afraid of are as weak, desperate, and vulnerable as we are.

# White Lightning

A rabbit and a crow were standing together in the street in front of my house. The rabbit hopped away as Spot and I approached, the crow flew up into a nearby tree, and I saw something lying in the road in the place where they had been standing. Saw with a sinking heart, since although I hoped it was just a piece of trash or food, I knew deep down it must be something living, or something that had been living. And sure enough, I realized when I got a few feet closer, it was a tiny brown baby bunny sprawled on its side.

The bunny looked as limp and boneless as a beanbag or a soft stuffed animal and at first I thought it was dead, but then I saw one of its tiny paws move a bit. I rushed into the house and yelled at Marek, who along with Spot was living with me in Iowa City then, to come out and help me with something right away. I left Spot standing in the kitchen still attached to his leash and ran outside again and by that time the crow was back down next to the baby bunny pecking at it with its beak. I shooed the crow away—it went back up in the tree, but only to the lowest limb, where it sat staring down on me with beady eyes—and Marek came outside and I went back inside and found a square shallow cardboard box to put the bunny in. I brought the box out and gave it to Marek, who said he thought the bunny's leg was broken. I glanced at it and agreed that its leg looked funny, and when we put it in the box it flopped and tipped and flailed alarmingly on its side. I left the rabbit in the box with Marek and went back inside to try to figure out what to do about it.

Nora and Stephan, Marek's fourteen- and eleven-year-old kids, who were staying with us for the weekend, came running big-eyed into the kitchen, wanting to know what was going on. Spot and our two cats, Madeleine and Marigold, were all in a tizzy too, Spot panting and wagging his tail and the cats rushing to the windows and staring out, quivering with bloodlust. The kids were excited also, though for opposite reasons from the animals, and rushed outside full of concern for the baby bunny. I felt totally riveted myself, galvanized, as if by the flick of a switch, into sudden, fierce rescue mode. All I could think of—all I could be sensible of, in some primitive, instinctive way—was that it was necessary to save this little living creature's life.

I went to the desk with the phone and started searching in the drawer for the phone book.

"What are you going to do?" said Marek, who had left the baby rabbit in its box outside with Nora.

"Call a vet, I guess," I said.

"Are you willing to pay a vet to take care of a wild rabbit?" said Marek, who at the time was full of anxiety about money.

"Yes," I said fiercely, for the moment ignoring my own money problems.

"If we leave it in the bushes it'll probably be okay," Marek said.

"I don't want to leave it in the bushes," I said, hardly paying attention to the conversation. I found the phone book and began searching through the yellow pages.

Stephan came inside as I was dialing the number of the only place that was still open—all the other vets closed at five-thirty and it was ten minutes till six—and said in an excited way, "Let's feed it a little piece of lettuce." I turned my back on him and Marek, held my breath and tapped my foot nervously while I waited for someone to answer.

Someone finally did and I told her the problem and she put me on hold, then came back and said that their office didn't generally deal with wild animals. Normally they would refer me to the animal shelter, she said, but since the shelter was closed now, she could give me the number of a woman in town who sometimes helps with the rescue of wild animals. The woman's name was Suzanne Hoffnagel and I called her right away. She picked up after the second ring, listened to my story, and said that we shouldn't pet the baby bunny or try to feed it. She also said that if we wanted to we could bring it over to her house, and then she told me how to get there.

I felt giddy with happiness, weak with relief. I don't know why the life of that one little baby bunny should have mattered so much to me when clearly there are millions of baby bunnies being born and dying every day, not to mention soldiers and citizens being killed by bombs and bullets, kids with bloated stomachs starving to death, people being murdered by their governments all around the world—but it did. That little bunny's crisis felt like an emergency to me; I felt as if some awful disaster was in progress, or had been in progress and I had found a way to stop it.

I shouted to Stephan that we shouldn't pet or feed the rabbit, who loudly relayed the message through the screen door to Nora in a slightly accusing of voice, as if *she* was petting and feeding the rabbit and should stop immediately, and then I went outside and told the two kids that I'd found a woman who said she would take care of the bunny. By that time Marek was in the bathroom, but Nora and Stephan and I stood there looking down into the box at the little brown thing flopping and struggling on its side, and breathed a sigh of relief. Especially Nora, who at fourteen was graceful and serious and loved animals at least as much as I did, and suffered horribly when they suffered. She held the box with the bunny while Stephan ran inside to tell his dad we were leaving to take the rabbit to some lady's house, then Stephan came back out, followed by Marek who wanted to come along too, and we all piled into my red Honda Civic and I drove slowly and carefully over to Suzanne Hoffnagel's, about five minutes away.

Suzanne Hoffnagel met us at the door and invited us into her kitchen, where there was a perfect little bunny-sized cage sitting on the counter. She reached inside our cardboard box and grabbed the bunny, who struggled in her hand, and placed it in a small cream-colored winter cap lying on its side inside the cage, explaining that the darkness inside the cap would make the rabbit feel safer. Then she asked us our names and address and phone number and wrote them down in a spiral-bound book. Marek asked her what she feeds baby rabbits and she told him they're allergic to milk and drink a kind of formula made of milk replacement for puppies, acidophilus drops, water, whipping cream, and pancake syrup. I told her Marek thought the bunny's leg might be broken and that we had also seen a little smear of blood on the newspaper in the box we brought him over in, and she said that she would check the bunny over later, but that its leg looked like it was okay, the bunny was probably just too tiny to be able to hop yet.

I also told her about the crow and the adult rabbit standing in the road, and she said that the rabbit was probably the mama bunny trying to protect her baby. She said the crow had probably stolen the baby bunny from its nest, and that once a crow discovers a nest it will go back for one baby bunny after another, so if we had time we should try to locate the nest and scare the crow away by squirting it with water or by banging on pans, and possibly rescue any other baby bunnies in the nest and bring them over to her house. She said to be sure not to harm the crow, which was only trying to feed its own babies. I paid careful attention to everything she said, and then

I thanked her profusely and said that I thought she was one of the heroes of our time and that if I ever had any money to donate I would give some of it to her.

She said that if I did rescue any more of the bunnies I should be sure to keep the lid down on the box I carried them in, since they could easily hop out and injure themselves by falling to the ground. I said I would, thinking of how I had carried our little rabbit from the car to her door in a shallow cardboard box with its top wide open. As I was carrying it I had glanced down into the box and gotten a good look at various aspects of its little body: its baby ears laid back against its head, its tiny feet attached to its little legs, its little brown sloping bunny rabbit head. I noticed that on top of its head was a tiny streak of white, like a little bitty white lightning bolt.

I called Suzanne Hoffnagel a few days after we brought her the baby bunny. I was genuinely nervous before I phoned her, afraid she would say the little rabbit turned out to be injured beyond saving. But she said that he was fine, the only problem was he might lose one of his eyes. "Crows do that sometimes," she said. "They peck out their eyes. His right eye is injured—that's what the blood you saw on the newspaper was from. I'm still waiting to see if he's going to lose it."

I asked her what happens to rabbits who lose their eyes, the ones who get rescued, and she told me she still releases them but she tries to find a safer place for them so they'll have a fighting chance at surviving.

I couldn't stand it anymore. "Why does nature have to be so cruel?" I burst out. "It seems like baby rabbits are the favorite victims of the natural world."

"That's why they make so many of them," Suzanne Hoffnagel said kindly. "But we still try to save every one we can."

The next time I talked to her she said she was hoping to release my baby bunny on Labor Day weekend. He had not lost his eye after all, and he was hopping up and down inside his little cage as if protesting his confinement. There was a piece of land on the edge of town where she had released rescued rabbits before—it had a shed and a clump of trees and a few other features that made it just a little safer than some other places where you could release bunnies—she was waiting for the go-ahead from the friends who owned the property.

I wanted to be there when she let my bunny go, but as it turned out I went to a Renaissance Festival with Marek and Nora and Stephan that day. When I called Suzanne Hoffnagel a few days later she said that she had indeed released my bunny on the appointed day and that he'd seemed quite happy, that he'd sniffed the air, hesitated for a moment or two, and then hopped off into the grass.

That was twelve years ago. Nora and Stephan have grown up and gone off to college and Nora has graduated from college and gone off to a different city. Marek's married to somebody else and Spot is no longer on earth. I live with Marigold and Meme, and sometimes I have Alice, a determined little rat terrier-Jack Russell mix who looks like a small Spot and has the same soft ears. Alice lives with my friend Rudy but sometimes she stays with me, and that's how I come to be walking her through the neighborhood on this June evening.

There are many rabbits in my neighborhood at this time of year. Last evening when I was walking alone I heard a rattling by some trashcans next to an apartment building and I looked over and saw a baby rabbit in the grass beside the metal cans: tiny, brown, innocent, frozen, afraid of me but oblivious of the cars whizzing past not far away, beyond the sidewalk and the grassy verge, on Burlington Street. Be careful, little bunny, I said silently, don't go in the road, and then I kept walking, feeling slightly worried about the baby rabbit, oppressed by its fragility. I turned down Governor Street, walked a little farther and saw another under a tree. And later, when I started my car and turned on the lights in my friend Sara's driveway after watering her plants because she's out of town—I saw a baby rabbit crouching in the beams of my headlights down at the end of the driveway, and I felt a stab of anxiety about that baby bunny's defenselessness, its delicate little bones, so easy to crush.

Now it's another evening and I'm walking Alice around the neighborhood. We've been around the block and are heading up Elm Street on the home stretch and it's getting late, almost nine o'clock, but there's still light in the sky because it's June. As we're walking along the sidewalk I see an orange striped cat running across a lawn on the other side of the street. It's a male cat—I don't know how I know that but I do—long legged and rangy, not very old. That's strange, I think, you never really see cats *running*. Then I see that there's a baby bunny hopping along the edge of the lawn and I see that the cat is heading toward her, he's *trained* on her like heat-seeking missile, and instinctively, without pausing to think about what I'm doing or whether it's a good idea, I pull on Alice's leash and we cross the road to try to head off the cat. The baby bunny hops into the street and the cat falls back as Alice and I come between them and then suddenly, startlingly, like a bolt of lightning arriving from heaven, like the angel of death itself, a big barn owl swoops down out of a nearby tree, lands on the tiny rabbit, grabs her in its claws, and carries her off.

The baby rabbit doesn't even scream, and when I tell my friend Jo Ann about it on the phone, she will say that that little bunny didn't feel a thing, that she probably died instantly when the owl stuck its claws into her, that the owl saved the bunny from a worse fate in the paws of the cat. I will think she's probably right, I'll remember reading something about small animals going into shock when they're threatened which keeps them from suffering, I'll think of how Susanne Hoffnagel said,

*That's why they make so many of them.* I'll think of all that and of anything else I can grasp at to try to make myself feel better. But I won't feel better. It will take me at least forty-eight hours to sever the thread of the mysterious connection between me and that little rabbit, to stop imagining her terror, anthropomorphically or not, during that merciless ascent in the claws of a predator. And it will take me even longer to come to terms with the facts that in this world cruelty might be a matter of perspective, that you can't save everybody or even very many but you can still try to save as many as you can.

# Invisible Geography

"Two hundred fourteen degrees northwest," the voice says. "One hundred twenty-three degrees northwest." It keeps going on like that, changing the direction every few minutes as the car negotiates the road. It's a male voice, clipped, slightly nasal, and it's coming out of the small rectangular machine Rudy's holding on his lap. It's a Hims, a little computer designed specifically for blind people. Rudy's parents gave it to him for Christmas and now we're using the compass in it as we drive to his parents' house. It has a word processor and a book reader and a bunch of other stuff too along with a GPS, but we don't need to use any of that right now, not even the GPS because we know the way. We don't really need the compass either but Rudy took out the Hims and turned it on just to hear what it had to say about the direction we're going in.

Rudy's parents live in Milford, a little town in Southwest Iowa about two and a half hours away from where we live in Iowa City. It's two days after Christmas and we're going there for two days. It feels wrong to me to be heading in this direction, west toward Rudy's parents whom I like but hardly know instead of east toward my sister, who is pretty much all the family I have left. I've visited my sister in other years on Christmas, although the painful truth is—it's painful to me in this moment—I haven't gone there much in recent memory. I've stayed home and attended brunches at a friend's house or gone to hotels with Marek and his children or done other stuff here in the Midwest instead of flying east, and my sister and I have talked on the phone: Merry Christmas, what are you doing today, what did you get for Christmas, did you like what I sent you.

Other than a few vague feelings of guilt I never felt bad about not being there with her before. She had her life and I had mine, I knew she understood that I had other things to do and didn't mind. She came out here one year when I was living with Marek and after that she said she was never going to travel again during the holidays. That's how I feel too: I hate the crowded planes, the delays and holiday misery, the cold and bleakness when you're driving to the airport. Another year when I was living with Marek we sent her a huge package full of clothes Marek had scavenged in consignment stores after my sister said she wanted a sweater or a heavy shirt or vest and used clothes were best. There were a couple of shirts in there that I found in another store but most of the garments came from Marek, including a slightly ratty flannel-lined denim vest that we almost didn't send because Marek was embarrassed by its condition, which turned out to be her favorite article of clothing for at least two winters.

All of that happened in the good years, when we thought we had all the time in the world left, when I thought I would be with Marek forever and my sister would always be in her house in Massachusetts, getting and sending me packages and calling me on Christmas. I thought I had all the time in the world left before this day came too, at least more time, enough time, to make my way out there, spend a month with her, be there with her when she left. It never occurred to me that she wouldn't want me to be there with her or that she was going to be leaving so soon.

Now, as we travel along this narrow two-lane road, I look out at the landscape—at the vast snowy fields on either side of us—and think again about how wrong I feel going west instead of east. I did try to go east when I opened up my email this morning, ten minutes before I was set to leave the house to pick up Rudy, take Alice to the doggy boarding place, and leave for Milford. I scanned down through my list of emails, answered two from clients, very briefly, and then I saw it: an email from my sister with the heading "sad news." I knew immediately what the news was, that she was going to be leaving soon, and not on any ordinary trip. I'd known all along that this was going to happen—she told me so herself, a couple of summers ago when I was visiting her, not long after she was diagnosed with ALS.

The disease was going fast, much faster than I'd imagined it would; even then, that first summer, her talking was slurred and she had to lean on a cane when she walked from the living room to the kitchen. "I've got some morphine for when the time comes," she told me, sitting cattycorner from me at the end of her long dining room table. My heart thumped painfully; the urge to weep wildly rose up in me and I forced it back down. I swallowed hard and said, "Well, I don't want to hear about it after the fact." I said the same thing last summer, when I was visiting again and someone who had dropped by the house to see both of us mentioned a device ALS patients use for talking on the telephone and my sister said, "If they live that long." At least I think that's what she said. By then it was hard to understand her.

"It bothers me when people just nod and smile when I know they can't understand me," she'd emailed me before that visit last summer. "If you don't understand something I say please let me know." And that's what I did, sitting cattycorner from her at the dining room table again. I'd been terrified to see her, wasn't sure I could face the shape she was in, but the minute I got there and she said something to me, her voice clotted and strained, the words distorted almost beyond recognition, I started laughing and she started laughing and I knew it was going to be okay. And every time during the visit, when I couldn't understand her, I'd look into her eyes, say I didn't understand, and we'd both start laughing. Still, I didn't stay very long. She said eating was exhausting and so was talking. At night when it was time for bed she said, "This is really hard and I need to do it alone." She went into the kitchen and from the living room I heard her gagging as, with great effort and strain, she swallowed some pills.

"I don't want to hear about it after the fact," I'd said one more time, earlier that day last summer, when she talked about dying, and when I left her house the day after that I was sure that I would see her again, that I would get to spend plenty of time with her, at least a month, before the end, that I would be there with her when she breathed her last breath.

And now here I was hearing about it, two days before the fact. I called a travel agent to find out about special fares, then emailed my sister saying I had a strong desire to see her one more time, to be there when she left. "I'd rather you didn't," she wrote back—her daughter and her daughter's husband were with her, she'd feel more comfortable doing it alone with only them in the house—and I responded, "I totally understand."

I debated whether to stay home instead of going to Rudy's parents and decided there was no point in doing that: Why spoil everyone else's holiday celebration? And what difference would it make if I was with Rudy and his parents or at home alone? I didn't have a smart phone yet but Rudy's parents had an Internet connection and I could bring my laptop and email my sister from there.

It's nice to be in the car with Rudy on this day, heading for his parents' house. The heater's on and the sun is out and I feel comforted by his presence. As we move steadily across the southern part of the state I get a peaceful, settled feeling—a sense of belonging, of accepting and being accepted, being part of a *together*. The feeling seems to be located in my body, in the area of my stomach, right there beside the desperate churning sadness about my sister.

There's nobody on the road but us. We pass through little townships within minutes—there are car dealerships and Casey's general stores and not much else—and come out on the other side and keep going, past barns and snowy fields, lonely clusters of cows congregating by a fence here and there. At one point I look into the rearview mirror and see the entire landscape reproduced—the wide fields, the sky, the barn, the cows, all of it bisected by the black ribbon of the road. Somehow the landscape—what we've just driven through—looks even clearer in the rearview mirror than what I see ahead, and I think of how life is like that too: It's a lot easier to see where you've come from than where you're going.

There's no Internet at Rudy's parents' house. Rudy's mother just never uses it, she says sadly when we get there, and she had it turned off on Monday. She hugs me and says how sorry she is about my sister, sorry too about getting rid of the Internet—if she had known she would never have had it turned off at such a bad time. I understand, of course, it's just one of those things, but I feel the chasm between me and my sister yawn even wider. What if she sends me one more email and I don't get it? And then—worse, infinitely worse, a lifetime's worth of worse—I don't write back to her?

I go into the room Rudy and I will share while we're here, get my cell phone out, and call my friend Kathy. Kathy, who's been my friend since we were in the Writers' Workshop together in the 1980s, who came to Iowa City from North Carolina in 1991 after my fiancé committed suicide and drove me back down to North Carolina in a rental car—I think of us traveling through the mountains of Tennessee in an otherworldly twilight—who kept me company, made me laugh, put up with my cigarette smoking for three weeks, in the rental house she and her fiancé had near Wilmington, during that time—I call her and tell her that I can't email at Rudy's parents' house and I'm terrified my sister will send me a message and I won't get it.

"Why don't you tell me your password and I'll check your email?" she says.

I panic: I don't think I remember my password. But I tell her what I think it might be and she opens my email server and types it in and it works. I haven't gotten any emails from my sister and when Kathy checks my email again later and then every now and then throughout the day I still don't get any.

On Saturday night Rudy and I drive to a local truck stop. Rudy called them an hour ago and they said they have wi-fi and we're going there now because it's the last night of my sister's life and I have to, I have to, if I don't I will die, send her one more message saying good-bye.

It's cold and dark and I hate this town. We drive along the empty streets, past houses where people are sitting inside in their living rooms watching TV—in my regular life, whenever I look through the lighted windows of some house at night I imagine someone in there lying on a bed reading a novel, but nobody's reading books in these houses. Past the Family Dollar store—it's the only retail store in town and we've gone there twice today, once for butter for our post-Christmas Christmas dinner, once for batteries for Rudy's mother's little CD-playing boom box, so she can listen to the book he got her. Past a used car lot and an auto parts store, down a long dark cold empty strip with nothing on either side, and then there it is, looming out of the darkness: the truck stop—huge, garish, all lit up. It has four rows of gas pumps, a convenience store, a sub shop—you can see the counter through the plate glass window—and a restaurant named The Lucky Seven. I drive across the unpaved parking lot, jouncing through deep ruts and four-foot-wide potholes, and park my car smack in the middle, well away from the scattering of cars in front of the restaurant and the row of semis lined up, noses out, windows dark, along the fence over on the left.

There are a lot of people in The Lucky Seven—it appears to be Milford's main spot for nightlife—and most of them turn to look at us when we go in. It's as if everyone here shares my anxiety and alarm about my sister, and it takes me a few minutes to realize it's just Rudy's blindness these people are reacting too; I've gotten used to this happening in small towns in Iowa but tonight it's disturbing. Rudy holds onto my elbow and we walk over to the bar where a tall bald man is standing, looking like the person most likely to be in charge. I ask him about the wi-fi and he tells me the waitress will give me the password as soon as we get seated—there's a table being cleared now. Rudy and I sit across from each other in the big booth the guy indicated—it's right beside the entrance—and a waitress brings us menus. I ask her about the wi-fi password and she comes back with a word written on a slip of paper.

I put the paper aside for the moment and read the menu to Rudy: There are steaks and pork chops and some fried or broiled fish on the list of entrees, fried cauliflower, fried mush-rooms, and many other fried things for appetizers. I decide to get broiled grouper and Rudy does too and after we've placed our order and the waitress goes off to the kitchen and I've gone to the salad bar and collected some pale iceberg lettuce, carrot shreds, and cherry tomatoes in bowls for both of us, I reach for my laptop, turn it on, and try to get connected to the wi-fi in this place.

I try and try. I get one message after another telling me there is no connection, I have no connection, my server can't use the connection, and finally I give up and start to cry. Rudy says a few things to try to make me feel better and then he gives up and we just sit there opposite each other. He looks miserable, and anger bubbles up in me—anger at the restaurant, at my email server, at Rudy because he can't make me feel better and because he looks so miserable. Our meals come and we eat them, me still crying—the waitress looks really concerned now but I don't care. I text Kathy about what's happening and she texts me back saying she'll send an email to my sister for me.

That night, sitting on the bed in the guestroom in Rudy's parents' house, I tell Kathy what I want her to say to my sister: That I've asked her to send this email because I can't; that she, my sister, has always been one of the most important people in my life, that I think of how we were together during some of our most crucial moments, that I will miss her infinitely, immeasurably, for the rest of my life. Kathy hangs up, writes the email, calls me back and reads it to me to see if that's what I want her to say, and then she sends it. I feel better, just a little tiny bit better, because I got to send this email, saying goodbye. I go out into the living room and watch TV with Rudy and his mother. There's nothing on and so we channel surf and then Rudy's mom remembers that she has a couple of episodes of Jeopardy saved on her Tivo and she and I watch those while Rudy dozes in his father's armchair.

When I get home the next day, at about eleven-thirty a.m., I set my laptop on my kitchen table and open it right away and there it is: an email from my sister. She tells me how sorry she is to make me sad and hopes I won't be sad for long. "I always thought I'd be around to protect you," she says, among other things, "but then I figured out you didn't need that after you were a little kid." I cry and cry.

There's an email from another friend saying, "Maybe you could find out what time she's going to pass and have a little ceremony yourself?" I can't imagine asking my sister what time she's planning to die but then I realize it would be good to know and maybe she wouldn't mind if I asked so I send her a little email saying, "I feel strange being so separate from you when you're doing this. Do you have a target time so I can have a little ceremony all by myself?"

Then I call Kathy and cry some more. At one-thirty it comes to me that I should check my email to see if my sister responded to my question—I can't imagine that she has. I can't imagine that she knows what time she's going to do this, can't imagine that she's doing it at all; I keep thinking, hoping, that she changed her mind, decided to put it off, maybe just for a month or two; that's what I would do. I can't imagine what it must be like to count down the minutes to your own death, so deliberately and consciously, to stare down the awful path to wherever it is you're going, knowing you'll be leaving the bright specific colorful familiar place we live in here, in our bodies, to go there—if there is a there—soon. My sister told me she doesn't believe she's going anywhere, but I do. I do believe there's another world, and I believe that it is full of happiness and light and goodness and that maybe it's only Cerberus, the three-headed dog that guards the door, that is frightening and ferocious. But the underworld I'm staring at the gates of now on behalf of my sister looks dark, cold, terrifying.

There is an email from her. It says, "My time is shortly after 2:30 eastern time." That's what she calls it: My time. The email is signed, "Take care, be well, your sister." I look at the time on my laptop. It's 1:36 central time, 2:36 eastern time.

I go upstairs and sit in the green brocade chair in the corner of my attic study. This is the spot where I meditate every morning for twenty minutes. Now I sit here and cry, long and deeply, I ring the Tibetan meditation bell—the small singing bowl Rudy gave me for Christmas. I strike the rim of that little bowl with its padded mallet over and over; I ring it loudly, angrily, desperately. Eventually I stop that and I stop crying, because there's nothing else to do. I sit there in my chair for a while, miserable, emptied out, and then I pick up my phone and call Kathy.

I tell her what just happened and we talk about every part of it: what my sister did, how I feel about it, what my sister must have felt about it and on and on. This is what we do, what we've done for years: We make sense of life together, our lives, life in general, the good parts, the bad parts, the worst parts.

I say I can't believe my sister isn't here anymore, and then it comes to me that she was hardly here before, recently, because of the ALS, she was already more like a virtual presence than an embodied one; she could think and she could email but that was about it.

"Wait!" Kathy says when I take a breath, about to launch on the next thought I'm having about this. "Something really strange just happened."

She says that she was lying on her couch just now, listening to me, looking at the Christmas tree in the corner of her living room, and suddenly something was there. "It was sort of like light and energy," she says. "Like light reflecting on water. I think it was your sister."

I start to cry again. Then I stop and say, "Do you have any sense of what's happening to her right now?"

"She's moving," Kathy says. "She's going somewhere."

I should be comforted by this but I'm not: I don't want my sister to be going somewhere, leaving for some unimaginable non-place where I'll never be able to see her or talk to her or be in her presence again. My sister, with her earthy concreteness, her mouth-breathing sleep beside me in the bed when we were kids, her teenage precociousness, her wide flirtatious eyes, her comfort with boys and sex, her loud hearty laugh when she got older—all of that now is just light and energy, and I hate that.

But then I think: Isn't that what we all are, when it comes down to it? I try to conceive of her in her light-and-energy state, heading toward some antimatter world a few stations down on the cosmic radio dial, showing up in Kathy's living room along the way. I can't really imagine that, can't imagine my sister in this suddenly new, strange, immaterial state—there's something abstract about it that defies imagination—but I'm willing to believe it.

A few days after that I got really, really sick. It got cold here in Iowa too, horribly cold, fourteen degrees below zero one day with a wind chill factor of minus forty. For about seven days I had the flu and I coughed and coughed all night and because of the coughing I kept waking up and lying there in a half-waking, half-sleeping, nightmarish state. It's warmer here now, at least it was yesterday, and I feel slightly better. I feel like I've just taken a short trip to some hell, a terrible frigid place full of bleakness and sickness and the loss of my sister—and now I'm on my way back to the regular everyday world. It's wintry here, but the sun is shining and this world is still full of ordinary pleasures.

# The Deep Limitless Air

There's a bird in the chapel. Anne and I notice it as soon as we settle into a spot in the middle of one of the long wooden benches in the guest area. We're in the fifth row near the back. There are two other people here, a guy at the end of the third row and another guy at the opposite end of the second row—they're the only other guests besides us at New Melleray in this late-January, middle-of-the-week moment. They're both very devout; we saw them genuflecting and crossing themselves before taking their seats along the rows during the two services we went to yesterday.

The bird wasn't here yesterday though. It flies madly from one side of the ceiling to the other: a flash of white up by the rafters above the monks, swooping and circling, disappearing for a while—maybe perching on the ledge that runs along the edge of the ceiling—then appearing again. The monks' chanting seems to bring it out.

This is Vespers, the canonical hour that starts at five-thirty p.m. It's not thrilling like Compline, which starts two hours from now, at seven-thirty, where four monks stand in the middle of the floor and sing the 91st psalm in the dark and then everyone sits in silence in the dark and then the bell rings, long and slowly three times and then three times again and then over and over, loudly, exultantly, at the end. In Vespers there's chanting and not-so-inspiring singing; one of the monks gets up and stands at the podium and reads a passage from the Bible, today it's Paul's letter to the Corinthians, and then everyone says the Lord's Prayer.

I stare at the monks as they chant back and forth, two small handfuls of men in white-and-black belted robes, seated in rows of stalls on either side of the chapel. The expanse of granite-tiled floor between them is at least thirty-five feet wide but the chapel is much longer than that, so the effect is one of narrowness. We guests are all the way at the back, cordoned off in our area behind a black wrought-iron fence with a gate in it; they open the gate and let us through so we can join a line and get a little splash of holy water at the end of Compline. The last time I came up here with Anne, about four years ago, I told her that I didn't get any holy water as we were walking out of the chapel at the end of that Compline—somehow the drops all missed me when I got to the front of the line and bowed my head before the monk dispensing the water with a snap of his wrist; I said I hated it when that happened. And Anne walked over to the big square stone font at the back of the chapel, the two of us alone in there by then, stuck her finger into the shallow pool of holy water, touched her finger to her forehead, and said, hilariously, "We get our own holy water!"

Only one of the monks seems to notice the bird today, the youngish one with thick brown hair and wire-rimmed glasses who looks, at least from this distance—I noticed when I was up here however many years ago—like Jim Beaman, the fiancé I adored who killed himself in 1991. It gives me the strangest feeling to see that monk. It feels like some magic trick played on me by life, some sleight of hand where someone who disappeared from one world, shows up, surprisingly, improbably, in a different world. Although I imagine the monk himself might object to being viewed as a magic trick or a symbol of someone else. Once last year, when I was staring at him during one of the services, I thought I saw him glance my way across the expanse of the chapel and then look down at his lap, alarmed.

He raises his head now and looks up at the bird and I can almost hear him wondering, like a homeowner who has to do something about an unwelcome problem in the house, *How am I going to get that out of here?* He looks back down and focuses on the song they're singing and the bird flies madly back and forth above by the rafters. I can feel its terror and wretchedness at being trapped inside this place of man, its wild creature longing to fly freely through the deep limitless outdoor air, but at the same time it seems like the holy spirit itself up there, as if the monks have conjured it up with their chanting and their prayers.

When the service is over, Anne and I go down to the big empty dining room in the basement to eat dinner. The monks eat their meals in a different room; someone told me they're strictly vegetarian. A local woman comes every day and cooks for the guests. We collect our food on plates on trays that we move along the line cafeteria-style, serving ourselves what we want. Tonight there's chili with hamburger and cottage cheese and carrot sticks and miscellaneous salads plus desserts and home-baked bread and red jello. We take our trays to an empty table—all the tables in this big room are empty tonight, except for two, occupied separately by the solitary men we saw in Vespers—and eat our food and talk companionably.

After dinner I go back to my room on the third floor—Anne and I are the only ones up here, the two other guests must be downstairs on the second floor. I sit in the chair in the corner and prepare to spend a nice long time looking out the window. It's dark out there now and the Virgin Mary statue is glowing peacefully on the lawn, but when I sat here staring out the window before Vespers her light hadn't gone on yet and she looked like one more part of the bleak scenery. It was twilight then, everything black and white and gray: black tree trunks and branches in the foreground; ancient tall firs farther down the lawn, their top branches swaying wildly in the wind; the snowy lawn; more trees to the right. There were only two patches of color in the scene: an orange blaze of light between the branches on the left—the sun going down—and beyond the trees and the shadowy gray lawn, an expanse of something grayish steely blue. It must have been a snowy field sloping to the horizon somewhere across the road, but that blue seemed unfathomable—silent, beautiful, imbued with some divine mystery that I long to catch hold of, just touch for the briefest moment—and so did the light which suddenly appeared, traveling swiftly from right to left between the tangled silhouettes of trunks and branches, and then disappeared. It must have been a car on the road, although it was farther away than where I'd been thinking the road was: some person going home at the end of a long workday or coming back from a shopping mall in Peosta.

I close the blinds now and open my book: "The Kingdom of Heaven Within You" by Meister Eckhart, which I took out of the Iowa City public library to bring here along with my novel. The Meister Eckhart isn't anything I would ordinarily read, but I thought it might inspire me or help me achieve a deeper level of spiritual satisfaction or something, while I'm here. "All creation should be as nothing to someone trying to get to God," I read. "The soul must remain distant from all earthly things." I close the book and put it down on the wide black glossy windowsill. I don't know how to get to God and the kingdom of heaven, of course I don't, although I feel myself groping hopelessly toward them in this place. But I know I don't believe they can be found in some abstract something beyond earthly things. They're here, I can almost feel it, in the chapel and in this room and in the dining room in the basement, in that blue field across the street and the car lights traveling between the trees.

At twenty-five minutes after seven Anne and I meet outside our doors and walk down the long empty third-floor hallway, descend two flights of stairs to the chapel, and sit through Compline; I get a good splat of holy water right in the face at the end. Then we go down to the little room in the basement where they have a coffee machine and hot water and a glass jar with a screw-on top stocked with tan, mild-flavored cookies—those cookies are always there, always the same kind, another mystery of this place. We pour ourselves Styrofoam cups of hot water and sit across from each other at the big table in the middle of the room and talk about this and that—our lives, our loved ones' lives, the wild things we did as teenagers—while the monastery surrounds and encloses us, huge, shadowy, silent, nearly empty.

When my friend Tania and I used to come up here years ago after I discovered this place, we tiptoed around feeling guilty about making too much noise, eating too much food, sneaking off to go for walks in the morning instead of going to mass. Nobody was watching us, nobody cared what we did, but we couldn't stop worrying that the monks thought we were doing something wrong. My friend Tania called it Joan of Arc syndrome. I tell Anne about that now and we laugh. She and I and Tania too, when Tania still lived in the area, go to the same Al-anon meetings. Anne and I have sat in rooms and listened to each other talk about our lives, have watched each other grapple with losses and challenges and scary developments and come to grips with them and move beyond them to other problems and situations and overcome those, for almost twenty-five years.

When I read, in "The Silent Life" by Thomas Merton, that a monk is one who lives in truth, that when "saved from the painful necessity to serve his own will, the monk begins to see himself and other men as they are," and that "together monks embrace their united purities, of clean and disinterested wills," I thought of Anne and some of my other friends in Al-anon. We write out fourth steps, take responsibility for our parts in things, get real about our character defects. And we try to learn how "not to suffer from the actions and reactions of others," as it says in a pamphlet on detachment; we try, moment by moment, little by little, to let go of the painful urge to force our wills on others and on ourselves. I look at my friend across the table and think of all that now, and I think of how she and I, slowly and gradually over many years, separately and together and with our other program friends, have learned how to get our own holy water.

In the morning we strip our beds and leave our sheets and used towels in piles in the hallway outside our rooms for the cleaning person, because our retreat is over and it's time to go home. We go down to the dining room and eat breakfast, but we don't have time to go to the chapel for Terce to find out whether the bird is still there. Instead we load our suitcases into the back of Anne's van, get in and buckle our seatbelts. Anne puts the van in gear and we head down the exit side of the circular driveway. She pulls onto the road in the gray January morning, and as we drive away from the monastery toward our regular lives, the snow gets dirtier and the air gets thinner and dingier, filling up with work obligations and emails and voicemail messages and all the other pieces of the busy chattering everyday world.

The next morning, back at home, I sit in the green brocade chair in the corner of my attic study and meditate for twenty minutes, as I do every day, searching for the kingdom of heaven inside myself. Sometimes I find it there in the form of a field of light that opens briefly inside me like a sunrise when I listen to the sounds around me: the furnace exhaling through the vent, cars passing, a truck accelerating, someone's dog barking in someone's backyard, someone's wind chimes tinkling somewhere, various unidentified pops and creaks in the house. But this morning I find it there in the form of myself, which I envision traveling toward, approaching through an inner minefield of other people's energies and expectations, the threats they pose to me in my imagination, coming to rest at a place of peace and comfort which feels, in this moment, like my true self: fearless, steady, unassuming.

Then, just when I'm finishing my meditation, a ladybug appears suddenly on the arm of the chair beside me. Maybe one of those Italian ones, which aren't real ladybugs, and which arrived in Iowa in hoards a few years ago and were and still are everywhere: Someone told me that when a carpenter tore down a sheet of wallboard in their living room they found a wall-to-wall mass of them behind it. I wonder where in my house this one came from; the windows are closed and I don't see any cracks in the wall or anything; it feels a little as if she materialized out of nowhere.

I examine her closely. She has black spots on her head, a faded-orange cloak of wings. I hear minute clicking sounds as she walks back and forth across a tiny range on the arm of the chair, then she pauses as if confused about where to go or what to do next. I hold out my pencil and she climbs onto the point. I place the pencil on the windowsill, and she totters along its narrow length like a small tightrope walker. I look at her, feminine, diminutive, a possible harbinger of a plague inside my walls, and I think again of the kingdom of heaven—I think of how Catherine of Siena said, "The path of heaven lies through heaven, and all the way to heaven is heaven."

And when I go upstairs the next morning and find nothing left of the ladybug but a light dry little shell on the windowsill, her disappearance is an even greater mystery than the tiny mystery of her living self.

# Boobie in Paradise

I'm crossing a wide stretch of blacktop in the dark and the rain. There's a plane over there and I'm trying to get to it. I'm late and I've had to find my way to the airport on a confusing subway train in a city I've gotten lost in. I know I need to board that plane and I don't want to. Most of the time I don't even make it across the tarmac in the rain to get on the plane but sometimes I do. Sometimes the plane even starts to take off, or I'm in a seat waiting for it to take off. Mostly what I have, in this recurring dream I've had on and off for thirty years, is the dread, the darkness, the deep sense of knowing that I shouldn't, can't, fly on a plane to Hawaii, and if I do will die.

What did those dreams mean, I think as I sit in the real airplane on the flight from San Francisco to Maui. The flight was supposed to leave at eight p.m. and get in at midnight, i.e., four in the morning in the time zone my body is used to, and back home I had worried about whether I'd have the stamina for that long flight so late at night on top of another long flight. In fact, the flight from San Francisco to Maui was delayed and didn't leave until about twelve-thirty which means we'll get in at four-thirty a.m. Maui time and something like ten in the morning in Iowa. But as I sit here squished into my seat beside the window, which I've paid 35 extra dollars for, I find that I'm tired but I don't really mind.

There's a mother and daughter sitting next to me, the daughter in the middle seat, beside me, the mother on the aisle. I know they're a mother and daughter because after everyone had boarded and we were sitting there waiting for something to happen, someone else was in the seat on the aisle, a tall guy who looked like he might be Jamaican, and the woman who's sitting there now approached him and asked him if he could take her seat at the back so she could sit beside her daughter. The Jamaican guy sighed, looked at me as if voicing a silent protest, and agreed. I was annoyed too, at the mother with her insistent presence, the daughter jammed in beside me fiddling with the remote found in a little compartment in the armrest. But now that we've taken off and the plane has established equilibrium and we're gliding along in the dark somewhere above the ocean, I can understand why the mother and daughter wanted to sit together. They order things off the menu in the seatback pocket and eat and drink them, first one thing and then another, hummus, bags of chips, bubbly water, coffee, chocolate chip cookies; they buy TV shows and watch them on the screen attached to the seatback in front of the daughter, stupid comedies with fat guys tripping and falling and performing antics in dresses, and giggle as if they're the funniest thing they've ever seen. The mother's wearing a light cotton muumuu and a red flower in her hair. She asks me where I'm coming from when her daughter's in the bathroom and acts amazed when I tell her Iowa. She and her daughter live in San Francisco.

I try to find some movie or TV show to watch on my own screen but there's nothing that probably won't depress me, so I turn on the thing that shows the position of the plane advancing incrementally in a line toward our destination. The progress is agonizingly slow, it's exhausting and boring, but nevertheless as I sit here staring at that thing, occasionally glancing out the window where there's nothing but blackness and the blinking light on the wing, much farther out there in the dark than you'd imagine it would be, I think of how this really isn't so bad. It's actually kind of fun. Not as much fun as it is for that mother and daughter, but they're showing me what it could be. I think about those dreams again, and I feel liberated, even gleeful, that I'm here in this plane on its way to Hawaii and it's nothing like those dreams.


Now it's five days later and I'm walking on the beach across the street from our Airbnb house on Maui. The sky is blue, the water is deep blue, there are fat blue-and-gray-tinged clouds on the horizon. The waves crest and slop, the foam rushes in, the water recedes leaving a dark patch of wet sand gleaming in the sunlight. Over and over. Slap of wave, rush of foam, retreat of foam, dark stain left behind.

I've been walking here every morning since we arrived and I've seen some of the same people over and over: the guy wearing a Santa Claus hat, the woman throwing a ball for her dog, the dog rushing happily after the ball into the water, the surly young fisherman. I've seen couples arguing, couples holding hands and staring straight ahead as if they have nothing left to talk about, guys with big bellies bulging over their swimsuits, tan twenty-year-old blondes in bikinis.

I say hi to everyone who looks at me as I walk along the beach and everyone smiles and says hi back, except for the young guy with the two fishing poles stuck in the sand, who glowers and grunts in the screw-you manner of teenagers everywhere. I walk all the way to the dense scattering of lava-black boulders and the little rise sprinkled with palm trees, then turn around and head back. Ahead of me now, in the distance, the beach curves around to a spit bearing a tiny cluster of white high rises. And beyond the spit, jutting out into the ocean, is the huge emerald hump of another part of the island, its mottled green slopes half-covered with cloud shadows, a large horizontal cloud resting across the top obscuring the peak, a row of wind turbines marching up one side.

I stop and talk to a woman—fiftyish with glasses, short graying blond hair—who has a Yorkshire terrier on a leash. The little dog roots around in the sand as she informs me he isn't hers, she's house-sitting and dog-sitting. She says she's been here for two months; it was a hard year back home—in Charleston, South Carolina, she tells me when I ask—but she's going to have to go back eventually to take care of business, hopes she hasn't been fired. I say Charleston sounds pretty warm compared to where I live in Iowa and we say goodbye and I keep walking. Here in this beautiful balmy place so far away from home, it's hard not to think in terms of Hawaii versus Iowa, not to think that this is better than that, and for a minute I envy that woman getting to hang out here more or less indefinitely and wonder whether I should try to do that too. But it doesn't take me very long to think of her saying it's been a hard year, to picture her alone in someone else's Kihei Road condo with the air conditioning on, her only companion a little doggie that isn't hers. I quickly come back to what I've been thinking ever since I arrived, which is that in the long run it doesn't really matter where you are.

I walk along the sand staring out at the water and the sky, trying to be here now instead of in my head, trying to smell the air, see the water, feel the warmth on my bare skin in this Hawaii December. But I can't seem to stop thinking for more than a few moments, and what I'm thinking about is those dreams—how it's obvious they were related to my phobia of flying when I lived in Boston, many years ago now; how both the phobia and the dreams are probably about some fear of getting off the ground; how strange it is that some thirty years on into having the dreams I've been virtually plucked out of my life and flown to Hawaii for a vacation, at no cost to me and through no effort of my own.

Whatever those dreams were about—whatever combination of traumas and parental messages and self-imposed limitations those old fears of traveling and flying, of getting off the ground, were made of—I still can't figure out exactly what—they seem to be gone now and in their place is just this: not Hawaii as it was in my imagination, not even the perfect vacation, but just life. Life where you can move forward, go places, not be afraid of what everybody else isn't afraid of. I wonder what God is dreaming for me now, I once heard a famous African sports figure say, and I think about that now as I walk along this beautiful beach; I wonder whether God, Life with a capital L as I think of God, has brought me to this place, perhaps as a way to tell me my dream is about to change.

In everyday existence, life with a lower case l, it was Althea, my ex-partner's oldest daughter, who was responsible for bringing me here. Marek's four grown-up kids plus Althea's husband and baby were meeting up with Marek here for a six-day reunion and Althea offered to fly me here and pay for my lodging using credit card points and of course I said I would come. Marek and I are staying in a separate Airbnb house about ten minutes' drive from the kids', as we call them. He and I have separate rooms. He's married to someone else. It's been at least five years since we've spent any time together.

It's a couple of days before Christmas but it doesn't feel like December or any Christmastime I've ever experienced or fantasized about. It doesn't exactly feel like Hawaii either, Hawaii as I've vaguely imagined it. It isn't fabulous or glamorous, at least this part of Maui. It doesn't even feel like a resort, as Nora, Marek's younger daughter, said when we had a chance to catch up for a minute about what we were thinking. It's kind of like Ottumwa with palm trees, as Marek keeps saying.

Ottumwa is a small city in southeastern Iowa, where Marek spent a fair amount of time when he was married to Maria, his fourth wife and mother of three of his four grown-up children who are here on this trip. Their mother was at least one wife ago, two if you count me, although Marek and I weren't married. But we lived together for a while, down in southeastern Iowa, in a town near Ottumwa, and I know exactly what he's talking about when he says this place is like Ottumwa with palm trees.

Nevertheless, I can hardly believe I'm here, in *Hawaii*, Ottumwa with palm trees or not, and I give myself over to the last hundred yards of my walk on the beach, to the warm air and the blue sky, the palm trees in the distance and the sand beneath my feet, and think about how glad I am to be here.


"Boobie," Marek says to me, when I get back to the house. When we were together we called each other Boobie, a nickname that evolved out of Baby, and he still calls me that, perhaps as a way of letting me know that although we're no longer a couple he thinks of me in the same affectionate way he used to, and because he calls me that I call him that too. When we were almost at the end of our nine years together, somebody, one of my clients who knew we called each other that, sent me a little hand-woven bag she bought in the Galapagos Islands, which had a picture of a bird and the word Boobie woven into the fiber. I remember staring at that bag back then, trying to imagine being free enough to go all the way to the Galapagos.

"Boobie, I hate America," Marek says to me now in the accent that is all his: Part Czech, part British English, with a little bit of a Boston accent thrown in. He and his second wife escaped from Soviet–occupied Czechoslovakia in the 1970s and he taught himself English in Boston listening to tapes of Bertrand Russell lectures and reading *The Phenomenon of Man* by Teilhard de Chardin. He no longer lives in the U.S. He's been carrying on the life of a homeless, more or less penniless, credit-card-charging jet setter for months now, going to Sydney, Tanzania, the Philippines, with a short stop in Buenos Aires. Such freedom to be transported around the world in airplanes, to go from one far-flung place to another, is unimaginable to me even in my current travel-anxiety-liberated state. Maybe I'm not quite as ready to become a world traveler as I've been thinking I was since we landed in Maui.

Marek's mind-bondage is about something completely different. He's been sitting here looking at Facebook and various news sites since I left to take my morning walk. "I hate this country," he says to me again, looking up from his computer, and I tell him grumpily that I *know*, he doesn't have to keep telling me. I know he hates America and it's fine with me. It no longer bothers me like it did when we were a couple, when I worried vaguely that his discontent would result in him moving someplace I wouldn't want to follow him to. Not to mention that it was just plain hard to be around all that *dissatisfaction*.

I used to argue, to get endlessly annoyed by those conversations, but I've learned to ignore them, and besides, he's not my partner anymore so it doesn't matter that much what he says. So I shrug and find the granola in the refrigerator and pour some into a bowl and dump the last of the vanilla soymilk, which the kids bought for us in the San Francisco airport, onto the granola and then I find a spoon. Marek says he's going to go out and cut a coconut off the tree on the front lawn. When we were coming back from a walk yesterday we ran into someone who lives in one of the other cottages in this little compound, a woman named Priscilla, whom Marek insists on referring to as Prissy—when I told him not to call her that because it means something not very nice in English and you can't just give someone a nickname anyway, he looked a little hurt and said why not, and then he asked me what does Prissy mean and I made a face and minced across the floor because I couldn't think of any language to adequately capture the meaning. Priscilla gave Marek her Safeway discount card in case he went to the grocery store and yesterday she told us there was a machete near the shed and feel free to chop down and eat any of the coconuts nestling in a little bunch high up in the tree. There's a ladder beside the shed too.

Out on the lawn Marek eyeballs the coconuts and tells me he won't need the ladder; he can reach one with the machete. He saws a coconut off the tree while I lie in the hammock rocking gently back and forth and then we go inside and Marek cuts up the coconut and some other fruit while I take a shower and do my morning exercises. Marek drains the coconut milk into two glasses and gives me one along with a fruit salad made with the coconut, chunks sawed off the pineapple that was sitting in a welcome basket on the table when we got here—it took him even longer to cut up the pineapple that it did to deal with the coconut, he tells me—and some reddish slabs of guava, from the guava that was also sitting, unnoticed by me, in the basket. We eat our fruit salads at the table with warm air coming through the window beside us. Marek says he likes the guava best, guava is his favorite fruit, and I say it's interesting how the coconut has almost no taste. Marek gives me a look like he can tell I'm straining to make conversation, which I am, but he doesn't say anything, and I think vaguely that it's a little sad to be spending time with him like this. With the weight and heft and heat of our relationship gone—love and all the effort and complications and illusions that go with it—all of that is gone and this is what we've got left, small talk about things like guavas and the non-taste of young coconut.

It's companionable, light, easy, and essentially meaningless, like an empty chrysalis or a dead palm tree branch that has fallen off the tree.

In the rental car on the way to the drug store, where we're going to pick something up on the way to the kids' AirBnB house, he starts talking again about Vladimir Putin. Somehow he's gotten the idea, which nothing can talk him out of, that Putin is going to hack into all the nuclear power plants in the U.S. at the same time and destroy America in half an hour. At least he was going to do that if Hillary Clinton had won the election. Now that Donald Trump is about to become our 45th president, Marek can breathe a sigh of relief; he no longer has to travel around the world avoiding the inevitable destruction of America, America going up in a huge puff of radioactive smoke, and he can come back and live in America again although he doesn't want to.

I can't blame Marek for being afraid of the Russians. When he was sixteen, in 1968, the Russians drove their tanks into Prague and took back all their power after the Czechs tried to wrestle some of it away during Prague Spring. When the Russian tanks rolled in, Marek climbed up to the top of a huge statue of St. Valcav's horse in Prague and stood there shouting a poem and nobody paid any attention to him. Over the coming days a father and daughter were crushed by a tank, a student set himself on fire in St. Wenceslas Square to protest the invasion, and Marek's brother was shot at by Russian soldiers and was never the same, spending his whole adult life in a mental institution. Czechoslovakia has always been in the crosshairs of history. Marek's father was forced to work in a Nazi airplane factory after the Nazis invaded the country during that era; he was caught sabotaging the factory machinery and the Nazis chased him to the rooftop and he dove five stories into the Vltava River below and swam away with bullets pocking the water around him. Marek tried to escape through the Iron

Curtain when he was seventeen, got caught before he made it close enough to the wall to get shot, and was arrested and sent back, avoiding a five-year prison sentence by being one year too young to go to jail and by his mother, who had connections, pulling some strings.

He and his second wife escaped together five years later after lying about where they were going to her employers at the Italian embassy. They could have stayed in Vienna after they got out of Prague but they were determined to come to America. They flew to Boston, received aid from a relief organization, got jobs in the same architectural firm. But America wasn't the good place they had thought it would be. And that's why Marek hates it so much, as he has explained to me on numerous occasions, told me at least twenty times when we were living together—he hates it because he thought it would be better than it is, not just another bureaucratic war machine like the Soviet Union. He hates it because he's *disappointed*.

Before the election he talked incessantly about the inevitable destruction of America at the hands of Vladimir Putin, blabbed on and on about it in his manic way with his Czech British-English accent, and everyone, every single person connected to him, his current wife, Natalie, who stole him away from me, and his beloved children, especially his older son Val, who is as sternly disappointed in him as Marek is in America, got so sick of it they stopped listening, stopped talking to him, stopped wanting to be around him, and unfriended him on Facebook. This reunion is an attempt to build the bridge again between him and his kids, or at least for them all to get together at Christmas. His wife Natalie, who might be the most mad at him of all of us, didn't want to come. His kids wanted Marek to have a friend here his own age and that's why they invited me. Plus I have relationships with all of them. My connection with Marek may have fallen by the wayside now that we're no longer the two boobies but my connections with his children have remained surprisingly fresh and vital.

Although Marek no longer believes the U.S. is a future radioactive cinder now that Donald Trump is our president-elect, he insists on talking about Putin and how he could destroy America in half an hour and how he still might do it.

"Will you stop saying that?" I shout at him finally in the car. "Nobody knows the future, not even you, Boobie!"

"You don't have to yell, Boobie," he says, suddenly restored to dignity.

But it's too late and I lose it. I start talking in a loud angry voice about Donald Trump and what an idiot he is, saying that Marek may be worried about Putin but what about Trump and all the damage he's going to do, he and his horrible cabinet are going to destroy this country and on and on, and that's what we're seeing, thinking about, living in now as we drive through paradise. We don't smell the orchids, we don't notice the pink bougainvillea growing in a hedge or see the wild roosters strut-ting up and down beside the road, crowing their pleasure into the early afternoon air. We are living in a country near the end of its life, on a planet close to destruction, in a place of darkness and despair, and no flowers or chickens or ocean or warm air can take us away from here.

It's Christmas Eve day. Val, Nora, and Stephan have gone on a long tour of the island in the rental van. There was talk at dinner last night about whether Marek and I would go with them, but they said they'd be gone all day, leaving early in the morning, hiking on difficult trails, perhaps to discourage us from going with them so they could have the time to them-selves, and everyone decided it would be better if they went on their own. I was both disappointed and a little relieved.

Marek, I could see, was just disappointed, but then he agreed that it would be fun to stay at the house with Althea, John, and the baby, so here we are.

Marek's sitting on the couch doing something on his computer, Althea and John are in the back bedroom trying to get the baby to go to sleep, and I decide to get a beach umbrella and a lawn chair from the shed beside the house and take them out and sit on the beach. I lug the chair and umbrella across a long stretch of lawn behind the house, then along a path that runs between a flat stretch of scrub. There are thorns in this part of the backyard, Althea told me, so you have to wear shoes. The chair and umbrella are heavy and awkward to carry along with my bag holding my book and sunscreen and by the time I get to the actual beach, a narrow strip of fine tan sand, I'm already wondering if this was such a good idea. It's windy and some gray clouds have blown up along the horizon and I have a hard time putting the two pieces of the umbrella handle together. Finally I manage to get the top part inserted a little way inside the bottom part, which I've jammed into the sand. Then a big gust of wind comes up and it collapses and the wind propels the umbrella part along the sand toward the water. I run behind it laughing a little, thinking of how this is like something out of a bad comedy. I catch up with it just before it blows into the waves and bring it back to my chair, and this time I manage to jam the top, umbrella piece of the handle hard enough into the piece of handle poking out of the sand that it stays in, although the whole thing lists to the side and the umbrella itself is almost on top of my head.

I sit there reading my book for a while, pausing a couple of times to reapply sunscreen on my legs, which don't fit under the shade of the umbrella. I decide this isn't worth it, I'm not really enjoying myself, but just as I stand up to take the umbrella apart, I see Althea coming along the path from the house, wearing a black wetsuit with pants that stop just above her knees and those beach shoes that keep you from cutting your feet on the coral on the ocean floor, carrying a surfboard. She says the baby finally went to sleep and she's going to try to do some body surfing if it's not too choppy out there. I sit back down in my chair and watch her carry the board along the sand and out into the water, waves slapping around her ankles. I go back to my book, and the next time I look she's farther out, still carrying the board under her arm, the swells rising up around her waist, then cresting closer to the shore. There's something brave and resolute about her, and I'm suddenly reminded of the contours of her childhood—of how when she was three years old her mother and baby sister were killed on the New Jersey turnpike when the whole family was heading to Washington, D.C., in a camper in the middle of the night. Althea's sixteen-year-old cousin, who had just gotten his license, was driving, having been instructed to drive only to the nearest exit while Marek joined Althea in the topper to nap because he couldn't stay awake at the wheel, and the cousin, who must've panicked, drove into a bridge abutment, Marek and Althea were thrown from the topper, the camper burst into flames and Barbara and May and the cousin who was driving all perished.

"Cause of death burns on 90 percent of the body," Marek once read aloud to me in a traumatized murmur from Barbara's death certificate, which surfaced in a pile of old papers when he and I were on the couch looking for some documents in a box; he swallowed hard and handed me the paper, stood up, and left the room.

After the accident he woke up in the hospital with a broken neck and Althea walked away without a scratch. She doesn't remember that mother, she said sometime earlier on this trip, she only remembers the step-mother who came after her. Althea is strong, competent, financially secure, happily married with a baby. She seems to have thrived in this life more than any of the rest of us, and I admire her for achieving all of that despite everything. I love her too, in some mournful way I don't quite understand, as if I detect the silvery strands of some mysterious connection between us, as if she and I grew up in different corners of the same dark fairy tale.

I go back to my book and read some more, and the next time I look up I don't see her out in the ocean at all. For a moment I panic. Could she have gone under and somehow not come up, despite her apparent indestructibility? I search and search and finally I see her, just a small head bobbing in the waves, way out by the horizon. I see her climb onto the board, get thrown off, climb on again, turquoise waves crashing around her, the sun sparkling on the water now that the sun has come out again. The next time I look up she's wading through the foamy waves close to the shore, carrying the board. She tells me the current was too strong out there to get anywhere. We exchange a little small talk and then she heads back to the house.

I get up and walk along the beach, leaving the chair and the umbrella behind, my bare feet slapping the wet sand at the edge of the water. I run into a good-looking couple in their thirties, the man wearing cut-offs and a t-shirt, the woman in a halter top and running shorts. The man tells me to be careful of bees. There are dead bees in the sand, bees that died on the green hump of land across the bay and float over here, carried on the waves, and lodge in the sand. They still have their stingers, he tells me, his wife just stepped on one a few yards back and got stung. I believe him and I don't want to be stung but I can't bring myself to look down for any stray bee that might be lurking in the sand, and besides, how would you even recognize what you were seeing if there was one there. I decide it's just one of those things, like so many things in life, where you have to take your chances, and I keep walking along, taking my chances.

I stroll along the empty beach, enjoying the warmth of the sun on my face and arms, staring out at the water and the blue sky. Just when I'm about to turn around and head back I see an unusual something, a big gray-green blob at the edge of the sand away from the water, where the beach ends at a wooden fence. I walk closer to investigate: It's a giant sea turtle, resting in the sunshine with her head turned sideways; I can see one side of her face, one large eye firmly closed. She looks limp and washed up, as if she's been flung here by some cataclysmic event or maybe died of old age or some toxin in the water. But then I see that one large eye open very slowly and close again and I realize she isn't dead, she's lying here sunbathing, enjoying herself.

Back in the house, having made my way back to the chair and umbrella, collected them and returned them to the shed, I find Marek standing in the living room. He's discovered that the wall-sized window that faces the beach and the palm trees and the riotous backyard, opens—you can pull it across so there's a screen but you can also pull the screen across so one whole wall of the living room simply isn't there, and Marek has done that while Althea and John are in the bedroom with the baby. It's strange to stand there in the dim afternoon light of the living room and look out at the bright airy shouting presence of the natural world and know that there's nothing between you and it, strange and not entirely pleasant. But Marek loves it. When I tell him I think he should close the window, he says he wants to leave it open so Althea can have the experience of feeling free, like there are no walls, and that will make her learn something about how to live, something he thinks she needs to know and doesn't know now. I tell him I don't think she'd like having that wall open to the air, who knows what will come in, maybe a bird or mosquitoes, and that I'm pretty sure she's more concerned with the welfare of the baby right now than she is about walls and freedom. But Marek is in some kind of trance of his own involving Althea, not as she is now, a mother with a baby and a husband, but Althea as the child and then the young woman he raised and tried to mold into a woman who would be happy joyous and free according to Marek's lights, and nothing I say can snap him out of it.

We wander through the window and out to the beach, arguing the whole time, walking along the way I've just come back from. Marek says he remembers now, the bad parts of being with me. He's been thinking it's nice to spend time with me here but now he remembers how I tried to control him and I try to say I'm not doing that but he can't hear it and I close my mouth and seethe. Then I pause and send Althea a text. *Dad wants to leave the big window in the living room open,* I write, and a few minutes later my cell phone dings and I hear back from her: *Thank you. Please close the window.* Later on, after we've walked back the way we came and Marek has pulled that giant window across and we've forgotten about our argument and gone on to other things, Marek tells me, subdued and shame-faced, that he read online that there are mosquitoes with the Zika virus here.

He leaves that night. The kids and I and the baby have one more day, Christmas Day, before we leave on our night flight, and Nora and Val and Stephan and I drive around looking for somewhere to go and something to do. Everything is closed for the holiday, and finally we stop at Ho'okipa beach where a few surfers are braving twenty-foot turquoise waves. Stephan and Val go somewhere farther down the beach and Nora and I sit on a wall and watch the surfers trying to ride those huge waves. They seem heroic to me, out there in the rushing crushing killing turquoise water, trying to get up on those little boards and stay up on them for as long as they can. Mostly they fall off. Only one guy manages to climb on and ride an enormous glassy curling turquoise wave all the way in.

"He made it," Nora says triumphantly.

"I wonder what he'll do now," I say.

But the answer is already in front of us, and we watch that guy, long dark hair, black wetsuit, gather up his board and head back out into the ocean.

# Desert Vacation

## I

The Boy Scout trail slopes gently upward for a long way, just steep enough to make me pant slightly as I trudge along in the baking heat behind my friend Jo Ann. My breathing is the only sound, that and the sigh of the desert wind, the drone of an airplane high overhead, and the crunch-crunch-crunching of my footsteps on the sand.

This trail ranges over both low desert and high desert, as we've learned from the sign at the trailhead. There are no Joshua trees here and the clusters of enormous pinkish-tan granite boulders which are in many parts of the park are absent too, although we see a scattering of them up ahead in the middle distance, which might be a sign that we are actually moving from the low to the high desert even as we walk.

This is the second day of our vacation, the fourth year in a row we've spent two weeks in the desert in March, escaping from the tail end of winter. For the first two years we went to Tucson and hiked in Saguaro National Park. Then last year we found an Airbnb house in 29 Palms near Joshua Tree National Park and we liked that so much we decided to come again this year. We're even staying in the same house.

Last year we found a pair of underpants lying under a cactus on the left-hand side of this trail. Jo Ann lifted the underpants on the end of a stick and we examined them: purplish tan semi-see-through fabric with little flower appliques, I seem to remember. We decided they must've blown out of someone's campsite and been carried by the wind across the desert till they arrived here, which was probably true because by the time we passed the same spot on the way back they were gone.

We don't see any underpants today although I sort of wish we would to make things interesting. Instead there's nothing but cactuses and scrub bushes and other desert vegetation on either side of the trail, and every now and then you pass a large anthill on the path, a circular mound of dirt with a quarter-inch hole in it and many black or red ants coming and going busily through the hole. Early on in this hike we passed two women and two children, one of them, the only male in the group, crouching over one of those anthills poking it with a stick, the little girl hanging back, the two women smiling indulgently at the little boy as if he was doing something smart and interesting. "Red ants!" the little boy declared.

I walk along the trail, trying to pay attention to everything I see. I long to know the names of all these plants and cactuses and trees. Somehow it seems important to know what they're called, as if that would help me carry them home in memory when I go back to the chilly, gray, and possibly snowy March landscape of Iowa, but I don't. I only know what a few things are called—cholla, ocotilla, jacaranda, prickly pear; Joshua tree, of course—and I keep kicking myself that I didn't remember to pack the field guide to desert plants I bought when I was here last year. But I didn't, so all I can do is try to memorize the exact size and shape and color of what's there, perhaps so I can identify it all later: thorns and spikes and bulges and spears, slender white curlicues, small clumps of pale tan grass that look like scraggly beards, shy little square-petalled yellow flowers blooming less than an inch off the ground, spreading bushes with silvery bark and black lines like zebra-stripes across their branches, yuccas with their sunbursts of spears (there, I do know another name), something that has a totally dead-looking base like a pineapple topped by lettuce-green spikes, each spike with a dark-brown pointy tip like it's been dipped in chocolate or poison. Each plant poking up out of the sand individually, separate from the others, as if attached to a different part of a giant creature sleeping underground, like outcroppings of the proverbial elephant felt by the blind men.

We hike and hike, looking, breathing, the baking sun and desert wind mingling with the packed thoughts in our heads till there are open spaces among them, like one of those Magritte paintings of a guy with blue sky and clouds under his hat. Finally after we've hiked a long way we get to the place where the giant rock formations are. These huge boulders along with the Joshua trees are the main feature of the park. Last year Jo Ann and I walked among the boulders on other trails where there were more of them and they were closer to the path than they are here. They're enormous, some of them a hundred feet tall or higher, and they have rounded edges as if they've been whittled away for millions of years, sand-blasted by the wind, carved out by water back in the ancient time when they were given birth to by the earth. Each boulder is like an individual entity although they stand together in clusters, merged and attached and leaning into each other as if propping each other up. They're full of cracks and crevices, hollows and fissures; they've got tufts of plants growing out of them here and there, holes you can see blue sky through. Some of them have lines penciled along their curving sides, evidence, as we read on a sign beside a trail, of primeval scrimmages and tussles among the rocks themselves, shrinkage and compression, lava forcing its way along cracks.

There are shapes hidden in them. You'll be hiking along staring up at those huge granite piles and all of a sudden a small whale or a huge mitten or the rear part of a bear or a giant hand gripping the top of a fifty-foot tower of rocks will come into focus. Some shapes are unmistakable: a row of gigantic pebbles, three slanting slabs like enormous playing cards or Biblical tablets, a sky-scraper-sized ape with two round hollow eyes and a grimacing line of a mouth. But many things aren't so obvious, and Jo Ann and I pause on the trails to exchange observations. Sometimes we see human faces, or almost faces, lines like closed eyes, a nostril or two above a downturned mouth; in one place we saw four gigantic profiles of Native American Indian elders, their wrinkled foreheads frowning as they gaze out over the rocky valley.

There's something uncanny about those boulders. It's as if they're inhabited by sleeping giants, colossal titans trapped in granite slumbering in this place for millions of years under some magic spell cast by the gods or the earth, and you can feel the threads of their dreams as you make your way along the sandy paths that weave among them. Or maybe they're not sleeping. I can't get past the feeling, which I have in this moment on the Boy Scout trail and which will get stronger and stronger the longer we hike in this park during this vacation, that there's some kind of dim benevolent ancient consciousness emanating from those rocks.

We come to the part of the trail where the terrain changes. The path starts to ascend more steeply, there's a big dip where you go up and down and then up again, and beyond that are white limestone stairs like the stairway to heaven and then the trail climbs steeply through the rocks. We remember it all from last year: the stairway to heaven, the sandy dip—I suddenly remember how I slipped and fell there last year—a big black rock that curves like an ocean wave and looks like some kind of living-room furniture—Jo Ann says she tried to sit in it last year and it wasn't comfortable *at all*. We go farther than we did last year, way up into the steep rocky part, and then we turn around and head back.

It's late in the day and we think we've turned around in

time but as we walk along, hurrying now, on the downward slope, we realize that maybe we haven't, quite. The sun goes down beyond a mountain peak which is now behind us; I turn around and catch the last rays shooting into the sky like some dramatic light show put on by God. As we rush along we notice that we're walking in a big circular shadow. Outside the shadow the scene is still buttery yellow, everything illuminated by the late-day sunlight which glitters on the sand and lies across the cactuses and illuminates the deep purple mountains in front of us and the valley in front of the mountains, the miniature houses and roads and the hem of sand which lies at the edge of the town and the very feet of the mountains. All of that is still golden in the sunlight, but the path where we're walking and the desert surrounding it has turned dimmer, grayer. Pretty soon there's a blazing sunset behind us and to our left, three wide swaths of garish orangey pink painted across the sky, and the light around us continues draining away as we keep walking and walking, the distance farther than we thought it would be.

Then even the scene ahead loses its illumination and the gloaming descends. The cactuses and the sand, the bushes and trees are now touched with a kind of indescribable magic, as if the secrets they've been holding back all day are coming out into the air, becoming the air itself, and all the rodents, the snakes and badgers and coyotes are rustling and waking up and coming out too, because this is their time, not ours, and we rush toward the parking lot just as darkness descends, tiny strings of lights glittering here and there in the little town in the distant valley ahead of us.

II

It's late afternoon and we're hiking on the Lucky Boy loop trail. At least, we hope we're on the Lucky Boy loop. We took a right onto this trail after we hiked to the end of the Lucky

Boy trail (not to be confused with Lucky Boy loop), stopped at the very end and looked out at the Lucky Boy vista, turned around and walked back a quarter of a mile and then took a right instead of going straight.

These trails are in an isolated part of the park. To get here we drove a long way down a bumpy sandy one-lane road, turned off onto a cleared space, and parked beside some cactuses, our rented white SUV the only car for miles around. There are other parts of the park that are actually busy, places where you see many vehicles parked along the curving black-top two-lane highway that winds through the park's 750,000 acres, and in some places, like where the road passes Skull Rock and Jumbo Rocks, there are lots of hikers climbing on the rock formations, kids leaping perilously across crevasses, big black crows hanging around waiting for whatever food scraps the tourists toss aside. Those places are beautiful too; even the presence of people wandering along the side of the road and swarming over the rocks can't ruin the power to fill your eyes and take your breath away of the giant pinkish-tan boulders towering against the blue sky and the Joshua trees reaching their cactus arms up to heaven in supplication, as the nineteenth-century Mormon settlers saw them and so named them.

But there's no one here for miles around. You might as well be on some other planet as you hike along. It's just you and the trail and the view across the desert, the mountains and the giant boulders in the distance, the sand covered with its fuzz of green because it's March and the desert is halfway blooming, the cactuses, the tender green bushes popping up like hope in the middle of the trail, the Joshua trees reaching up to the sky.

That's how it was on the Lucky Boy trail, the first part of this hike. Even then it was late afternoon and there were shadows in the dips in the footprints in the sand on the trail. When we got to Lucky Boy vista we stood looking out at the view, our eyes filling with the sky and the distant bluish-purple mountain ranges, one range resting beyond another and then another and another, all the way out to the horizon like a vision of heaven. There was a rusted tin can on the ground among the cactuses as if left there by a cowboy a hundred years ago, a tiny purple flower blooming all alone in the sand for no one to see. The wind clanged in the metal sign attached to a wooden post. We paused there for a long moment, then turned around and walked back and took that right onto Lucky Boy loop, and now here we are.

We've been walking along the loop for a long time, much longer than it seems like we should have been. The first part of the loop trail was full of ups and downs, places where it looked like one of those paintings designed to show perspective, with a big hill in front and then another hill behind that, a Joshua tree in the foreground, mounds of black rocks in the background, the edges of everything crisp in the late-day sunlight. Then there was a narrow path that led between some of those huge tan granite boulders. Here, up close and personal—for a while the trail passes next to them with no space at all between you and them—they began to seem not quite as friendly and benevolent as they have until now.

By then we'd started suspecting that maybe we weren't on a loop at all but had somehow gotten onto some other trail that leads to nowhere, traveling on and on into the desert, taking us farther and farther to nowhere, past twilight into the night. And then we came to this wash, a flat wide trail where the sand is filled with tiny gray pebbles so your feet sink into the sand with every step, making it harder and more taxing to walk.

By now the sun is almost behind the mountains and the shadows have grown longer and it seems we're nowhere near the end of the trail, and Jo Ann starts to panic. She looks at me with wide-eyed concern as she stops and hands me my

Kind bar. Usually we rest on some flat rock when we eat these, but we don't want to stop right now, we're afraid to stop and do nothing while the sun sinks farther and faster behind the mountains. So we unwrap and eat our Kind bars as we trudge along, licking the chocolate off our fingers, folding up the left-over plastic packaging and sticking it into our pockets.

"I don't care, I've got to get the stones out of my shoes," Jo Ann says when we've gone another hundred feet or so. She perches breathlessly on the edge of a large flat-topped boulder and takes her shoe off while I keep walking. "Mary, what have we done?" she says when I come abreast of her.

I can see she thinks we're truly lost, that we're going to have to spend the night huddled on the trail surrounded by the inhospitable things of the desert, which hide in their holes and under bushes and in the creases of rocks during the day but come out at night, howling and slithering, celebrating and populating in the pitch dark. That she thinks we might even die out here, that maybe we'll never find the way home.

But I refuse to be afraid. I don't even actually feel afraid.

"Well, all we can do is keep walking and see where it takes us because we're not going to turn back," I say, wondering how long my cell phone battery will last if we have to use the iPhone flashlight to make our way along the path in the dark.

I don't know why I'm not afraid. I'm usually the first person to get scared of crashing or getting lost or dying, of crises and disasters of all kinds. But this time I'm not. Somehow I know it won't come to lighting the way with the flashlight on my cell phone, that we are on the right trail after all, the Lucky Boy loop like it said on the sign where we took that right back near Lucky Boy vista, and at any moment we're going to see the original trail we split off from, which will take us to the car.

And that's exactly what happens, except that instead of coming to the right trail we see the road itself. First we see the roof of a silver car glinting momentarily in a spear of sunlight, moving along the invisible road between the cactuses up ahead like a shark fin traveling along the waves, and a few yards on we see the road itself, the sandy road we parked our car on. Our car isn't there. We've come out in a different spot than the spot we parked in, and as we walk along the road to our SUV, which is way, way up ahead, tiny in the distance, we're exhausted but happy and relieved, proud of ourselves for hiking so far and a little bit changed by getting lost on the trail and continuing anyway and coming out on the other end.

## III

It's our last day here. Things that weren't blooming when we got here are blooming now, orange bells on the long stem by the corner of the house, a single yellow flower beside the pavement, a whole prickly pear's worth of tissue-y pink blossoms. I've almost gotten used to it here, to the point that it's shocking, unimaginable, to think of ice and snow and cold back in the places where we're going. It seems more normal to sit in a blue metal lawn chair in front of the house watching a hummingbird arrive at the feeder, pause in midair as if looking out across the view, light on the rim and tilt abruptly to poke its beak into one of the holes for a sip of sugar water, straighten, stare, sip again, then whir off across the yard. To see the top of the palm tree, its green leaves glittering and shifting in the sunlight, begin to flare and whip in the wind, the sand begin to swirl at its feet, twisting and turning into a miniature tornado that rises ten feet into the air, then drops back down as the wind drops, the specks of sand settling onto the ground again.

The hummingbird feeder and the palm tree are at the front of the house and right now I'm on the patio by the backdoor. It's around two o'clock in the afternoon, hot but not too hot, breezy, almost windy. I'm sitting in the shade of the desert willow tree, its long trailing branches covered with elegant spear-shaped leaves, the leaves themselves holding tiny hidden yellow flowers; sometimes you'll find one of those little flowers on your plate while you eat breakfast out here or nestling in your hair. The big black Italian bumble bee is droning endlessly, circling the willow like it always does as if searching for something, getting closer to the tree, then farther away, then approaching again. Jo Ann calls it Chef Boyarbee, picturing it with a little white chef's hat and a comical mustache. It was here last year too or maybe one of its relatives; there's a hole in the sand by the driveway where I think they live.

Yesterday he flew directly across the patio toward me, stopped two feet in front of my face, hovered there for a second as if examining me as I've been examining him for almost two weeks now, then turned and dashed away. Chef Boyarbee is in a bad mood, I told Jo Ann afterwards, when I found her sitting in the blue metal chair in front of the house, her feet up on the other chair and her laptop open on her lap, a glass of iced tea on the table beside her.

At least we know he survived. A few days ago we saw him or one of his brothers or sisters resting on a striped dishtowel we'd hung on the clothesline along with the rest of our laundry. Jo Ann tried to pry him off with a stick but he was stuck, even a few strong nudges with the stick wouldn't budge him and we thought for sure he was dead. But when I got up the next morning and went out there to look he was gone. He must've been clinging stubbornly to the dishtowel, sipping moisture from its fibers.

I sit at the table idly watching him circle the tree, the stiff warm breeze lifting the long trailing willow branches and the hair on the side of my head. I love this place so much I long for it desperately even while I'm here. Especially when I'm here, because once I get back to Iowa it will grow dimmer, receding along the corridors of memory until it's more like a shadow than this vivid place full of color and sounds and air. I dread going back to regular life, to cold gray weather and relationship issues and not enough time, one day passing unnoticed after another, life fading out of one season and into the next. While I'm here I keep forgetting about the good stuff, my house, my cats, my friends, my town, home with all its comforts, spring on its way. I won't remember any of that till I've been home for a few days.

I look at my laptop and try to focus on my writing. But it's hopeless, and I'm sitting here staring off into space when something sort of surprising happens: An orange butterfly shuttles quickly into the yard from the right as if shoved by the invisible hand of the wind, lands on the sand about seven feet in front of me, stays there for a few moments as if shaking herself off and collecting herself, then rises unsteadily and potters over the edge of the roof.

I get up to go in the house to tell Jo Ann about the butterfly. But before I go inside I pause at the backdoor and take one last look around. I look at the mailbox at the end of the driveway and the distant mountains across the street, at the bricks in the patio and the cactuses in the front yard, yuccas and chollas and a million other things, and that deep green oleander tree outside my bedroom window, which casts its moving shadow on the wall in the daytime and touches the screen with one of its branches, getting in the way so I can't close the window and I have to sleep all night with the cool air making its way into my dreams.

# The Praying Mantis

There's a four-inch-long praying mantis on the screen door of the hermitage.

A few minutes ago I pulled up behind this little house, crossed the grass beside the solar panels thinking that everything looked so familiar it almost felt like home, stepped onto the deck and let myself in, pulling the screen door shut behind me. I took the curtains off the windows to let in more light and rearranged the furniture, shoved the armchair aside, put the battery-operated boom box on the floor at the foot of the bed, pulled the table in front of the double French-style windows—everything like I had it the last time I came here.

About six months ago I decided I wanted to go someplace where I could write for a stretch without interruptions. I asked around and searched the Internet and found this, a hermitage in a Franciscan spirituality center not too far from where I live, and reserved it for a week in September and a week in October. I got a lot of work done in September, went for long walks when I wasn't writing, cooked meals in the tiny kitchen, practiced being alone for five days in a row.

And now here I am again.

A minute ago I pulled the chair up beside the table, sat down and looked out, knowing I had to go back and get my stuff out of my car but thinking I'd give myself five minutes first to get acclimated. That's when I saw it, that giant praying mantis, resting on the screen upside down and at an angle.

I sit here for a few moments, thinking maybe it'll fly away. But it doesn't show any inclination to go anywhere so I get up and get the broom from its spot beside the refrigerator and whack the edge of the door frame on my side, thinking maybe I can scare it away. It doesn't even stir. I sit back down. I'm afraid to open the door and walk past it to get my stuff out of the car. What if it whirs into my hair or comes inside the house?

So I sit here trying not to think about a New York Times article I read not long ago, in which the writer described watching a giant praying mantis perched on the edge of a hummingbird feeder grabbing a hummingbird and eating its brains. A picture accompanied the article. That praying mantis looked just like this one. There must be more of them around these days than there used to be. A few weeks ago, when my friend Rudy and I were out walking in the evening, I saw a young couple ahead of us staring at something by their feet. The couple moved on and I saw a praying mantis resting on the sidewalk—green, two inches long, wings folded. Then just as Rudy and I came abreast of it, it flew up into the air. I ducked but Rudy, who's blind and couldn't see it coming, didn't, and it passed over his head just inches away.

I try not to think about that too as I sit here waiting for this one to fly away. I wait and wait but it still shows no inclination to go away and I have to get my stuff out of the car. So finally I get up and slide the screen door across very gently, very slowly; I exit quickly, close the screen and go to my car and get my stuff: There's lots of it, enough food for five days packed in two cloth bring-back bags; a suitcase, a tote bag with my laptop and manuscript and kindle and two regular library books, a down comforter and pillow. I pile all of that on deck. The praying mantis is still there. It looks like it might have moved a half inch or so and now it's resting on its forelegs, its back bent and its head raised as if it's looking around the yard.

"Hello, pal," I say in a conciliatory way, then very slowly I slide the screen door across, rush inside with all my stuff, and close the door behind me.

And now here I am, back in my chair, watching it. It appears to be watching me too. To be curious about me. It moves slowly around the screen, an alien with long wings, a skinny neck, a bulbous head, and wraparound eyes. I have all the time in the world to watch it, and although its presence, its very being, makes me shudder, I begin to feel contemplative as I sit here staring at it. It seems contemplative too, curious, silent at the core of its alien being, and when it eventually walks slowly across the screen, pauses at the very edge, and disappears—I don't see it fly away but it must have because when I go outside to look it's gone—I feel almost disappointed.

# The Couch

I'm staring at the laptop on my kitchen table, talking to a client about her writing. Every once in a while I notice the sounds in my living room—no scraping or groaning or crashing, just small sounds, something being moved followed by a long pause, then a little more movement, another pause. I go back to my work and forget about it.

Marek, my partner of nine-and-a-half years and now my ex, is here, helping me move my couch, which I'm about to replace with a newer nicer couch—at least I hope it's nicer. He's going to take the old couch out to the curb so it can be picked up tomorrow by a guy in a truck from the Iowa City waste department and hauled off to the dump. Marek said, before I started coaching—the appointment was fixed and he arrived about ten minutes before its starting time—that he was going to bring the couch through the kitchen because he didn't have his dolly with him and it would be too hard to get it down the front steps. I don't know what he's doing in the living room now and I'm not really thinking about it—I'm thinking about what my client's saying to me and what I'm saying to her— but in the back of my mind I keep expecting Marek to come through the kitchen with the couch at any moment.

When I finally finish up and go into the living room, the couch is gone and Marek's nowhere around. I find him in the bathroom, sitting on the edge of the bathtub reading this month's issue of the AARP magazine, which I've left in a magazine holder along with the last few month's New Yorkers.

"Where's the couch?" I say. "I thought you had to bring it through the kitchen."

"It's outside on the curb," he says. "It turns out it was easier to get it through the living room door."

I'm momentarily shocked that all that happened while I was in the kitchen not paying the slightest attention, that Marek somehow managed to get the couch through the living room, down the steps, and onto the curb, alone, without a dolly, and it wasn't even that big a deal. I thank him profusely and he just shrugs, kisses me on the top of the head, and leaves to do some urgent errands.

I go into the living room and look out at my couch sitting there on the curb. I feel enormously relieved that it made its way out there so easily, that what I thought was going to be a big ordeal, one of several involved in getting a new couch— I'm always surprised whenever I buy some new big thing by how hard it is to implement the change—wasn't. It pleases me to no end that I didn't have to be involved in this particular moment of heavy lifting, not that I would have literally lifted the couch, but I would have lifted it psychologically, metaphorically, while someone else was doing the lifting, me standing there feeling responsible because so much work was being done on my behalf. But that didn't happen this time, there are no strings attached. I don't feel guilty about Marek doing me a favor, don't have any feelings one way or the other about him or the fact that we've broken up or anything else. I just feel grateful that he was here helping me, grateful that we can still have a civilized friendship.

But I do feel, standing there looking at my couch through the window, the couch sitting on the verge, looking forlorn and legless—Marek unscrewed its square wooden legs and took them with him for some unspoken purpose—a deep irrational pang of sorrow on the couch's behalf.

I know it's stupid, the ultimate act of projection and anthropomorphism to feel sorry for a couch, but I can't help it. I turn away from the window and make myself stop thinking about it, not because I don't feel the feeling very strongly but because I know if I dwell on the feeling it could become unbearable. And because I know I'm just projecting my own feelings onto something that has no feelings of its own—right?—so what's the point?

The woman from the waste department told me the truck would arrive and pick up the couch first thing in the morning, and as soon as I get up the next day I go into the living room and look out the window, filled with a strange sense of expectancy, to see if the couch is still out there. It is, sitting on the curb, the two long cushions that form the back looking flattened and squished, the whole couch looking a little ruffled and windblown from its night spent sitting out on the curb among the dry fall leaves and layer of icy snow and unseasonable November cold.

I've always loved that couch. The fabric is pale mint-green twill with tan piping around the edges. I bought it from Montgomery Ward when they were about to go out of business and it's served me well: I've taken many naps on it, I sat on it with Marek the night we got together, the two of us parked there talking for hours about his family and my writing and a million other things. But over the last couple of years it's gotten ratty. My cats loved to lie on it in the afternoon sunlight and the two big pillows that created the back got hopelessly squished and started developing tears from the cats' claws; at first they were small almost unnoticeable rips but they grew over time, and the fluffy white synthetic-fabric stuffing that filled the pillows started to peek out through the rips, and then Alice, my friend

Rudy's puppy, started pulling it out and spreading it around the room and even eating it.

Clearly, it was time to get rid of the couch. Still, I felt irrationally bad about doing that. I tried to find some way of giving it a new life, partly for environmental reasons—I felt guilty about contributing a big item to the landfill—but mostly, if the truth were known, because of my strange couch codependency. I called a couple of places to see what it would cost to have it reupholstered—even getting those pillows fixed would cost almost as much as a new couch, I learned. I flirted with the idea of trying to sew new upholstery myself but knew that even if I bought the fabric and arranged to borrow my friend's sewing machine, I'd never do the work. I looked into whether I could donate a damaged couch to our various charities and found out I couldn't. Then Slumberland had a big sale, I bought a new couch to replace the old one, and here I am.

At ten-thirty the truck finally comes to pick up the couch. First I hear it idling outside, then I see it through my upstairs window: There's a guy out there loading my couch onto a lift attached to the back of a white City of Iowa City truck. He pushes some button and the couch is lifted to the level of the truck bed and the guy shoves it in next to a queen-size mattress. The guy gets into the truck and I watch as my couch suffers the indignity of being driven away, alone, abandoned, unloved, crammed in ignominiously next to a mattress, and my heart is breaking.

Now I'm waiting for the new couch to come, hoping I like it as much as I thought I did when I saw it in the store.

# Insomnia, Dreams, Reflections

It's six-thirty in the morning and I'm lying in bed trying to go back to sleep. I tried to make myself go back to sleep at three too. That time I tried to do it by employing my secret mantra weapon. Every time I wake up in the middle of the night I say *I'm going back to sleep right now* over and over, in my head, and it actually works about seventy-five percent of the time. But it didn't work at three a.m. so I did the thing I do when it doesn't work: I got up and did stuff. I vacuumed my living room rug, did some dishes, answered some emails, and read for a while.

But I have to go back to sleep now if I'm going to have a hope of having a normal day, so I'm lying here trying—trying *again*—to do that. Usually I fall asleep really easily after I've been up puttering around for a couple of hours in the middle of the night, but this time it's not happening, so far. I'm wearing a sleep mask to keep out the light but even though it's dark in here under my mask I can still feel morning occurring out in the world, cars whooshing by on the road, birds twittering, the yellow morning light getting stronger by the minute. My cat Meme is snoring quietly on top of the pillow on the other side of the bed, her friendly furry insistent presence both comforting and exasperating. A little while ago she was licking her leg making loud slurping sounds, shaking the bed slightly, and without forethought I snatched the sleep mask off, sat up, and hollered at her: *Stop that!*

*You're bothering me!* I added, as if she could be reasoned with. She stopped, foot poised in mid-air, and stared at me looking confused and slightly hurt, then let out a few tentative purrs. I lay back down and put the sleep mask back on and here I am, ten minutes later, fifteen minutes later, half an hour later, still not going back to sleep.

I keep thinking, thinking, thinking about stupid meaningless things, what I'm going to make with what I bought in the grocery store last night, what I said to so and so yesterday and blah blah blah. This, that, this, that, on and on, without my having any control over it or barely even noticing it. If I could make a little window of emptiness inside my thoughts I could probably go in there and fall sleep and I've decided to try to do that by meditating.

So I've got my cell phone set to Insight Timer, the meditation app I use, and every now and then it dings quietly, a pre-set reminder to empty my mind. The ding barely penetrates my thinking about this and that and there might be some times when I don't notice it at all. Every now and then I remember that I'm meditating and I try to sweep my thoughts to the side of the picture with a little mental broom, and when I manage to do that and hold onto non-thinking for a few seconds I listen to the sounds around me: those cars whooshing by on the road, my cat's tiny snores, various creaks in the house, that quiet Buddhist ding coming every now and then from my cell phone.

Then it happens, during one of the moments when I'm briefly achieving inner silence: A trap door opens inside my mind. I fall a little way down into the opening and maybe something comes up through it as if to meet me. In the opening I find a scrap of a dream that I keep having in various permutations about my sister. In waking life Christine died about two and a half years ago, and ever since then I've been dreaming about her almost every night.  In the dream she's a teenager and I'm with her in her old childhood bedroom in my parents' house and she's sick and I know she's sick and the whole dream is suffused with the feeling of that, there's something terribly wrong with her.

I don't know why my dreams have to show me this over and over almost every night, who or what is showing it to me: I sort of like to think that our dreams come from some presence like the guy behind the curtain in the Wizard of Oz, that on the other side of the elaborate tapestry of our daily lives there's somebody, maybe a different somebody for each of us, pulling levers and turning dials, making up dreams and inserting them into our minds at night to show us what we're supposed to be learning and doing here in the world. That sometimes when they're too busy to make up a new dream they pop in a DVD of an old dream and that's why we have those recurring dreams.

But I have no idea what that guy is trying to tell me with these dreams about my sister. They aren't really what interests me anyway. It's that world down there inside me on the other side of the trap door.

I lie here on the bed with my sleep mask on, waiting to be pulled down deeper into the world of dreams, for the trap door to open wider and for me to descend through it, spontaneously, through no effort of my own. But that doesn't happen. Instead I start thinking again. I think about that world down there on the other side of the door. An image on a tarot card, the Moon, comes to me, maybe because today, after I go back to sleep and wake up and get up again, I'm going to be playing with the tarot cards, which I do once a month, with my friend Tania, who taught me how to read the tarot about twenty-five years ago and with whom I've been throwing them ever since. These days we do it long-distance over the phone, and I texted her about ten minutes ago to tell that I'm planning to go back to sleep but I haven't yet and we might have to push the time back and I'll text her again when I wake up.

The Moon in the tarot has to do with dreams and mystery and the underworld, as Tania and I remind each other whenever it shows itself during one of our readings. In the image there's a kind of opening with two dog soldiers on either side, the Ra kings of ancient Egypt, guarding the door; beyond that is a passageway and at the end, partly visible inside an oval, is the moon, blue and green and marbled, with a few lines of red. It looks like the earth, and I lie here thinking about that, how the underworld is just another version of the earth. I think about other things related to the underworld too, as I lie here not going to sleep, about how I read recently that in certain ancient traditions the afterlife is depicted as taking place under the ground, not just hell but heaven also. I think of how that's sort of my idea of the afterlife too, somewhere you travel to along a passageway that starts in your consciousness and goes down instead of up, the way you fall sleep and descend into the world of dreams. I think of how the things I've read about the afterlife all say that—that the afterlife is really a big out-picturing of your consciousness and this world is too, sort of, although we don't know it. I think about those dreams I have where ugly creatures, huge scorpions and enormous slimy insects with wings and pointy protuberances are sitting on the edge of a large hole in the basement as if they've crawled up out of the sewer of ugly feelings in my unconscious. I think of how I sometimes dream about lions that come into my house, entering through the backdoor and coming into the kitchen and walking around; in the dream they tolerate me, they even kind of like me, but I know that they could turn on me at any moment. When I throw the tarot cards later in the day with Tania I will get four different cards that have pictures of lions on them, and I will think of how the cards are like dream symbols themselves, how they somehow bridge the gap between dream-ing and waking, real life and symbolism, and at the same time are just a series of indescribably beautiful pictures on rectangular pieces of cardboard sitting in a cloth bag in my house.

I think about all of that and more, this that this that, and then finally I descend into sleep, quickly, quietly, without noticing, at a moment when I'm not paying attention. I don't dream about my sister. My dreams are full of clashing incom-prehensible thoughts and images and scraps of stories about a bunch of nonsensical this and that. Jo Ann shows up in them somewhere. And you're in there too, as you often are. Mostly in my dreams about you there's nothing much happening, just a lot of swirly, inchoate feelings. When I wake up today again, at ten minutes before ten, I'll think about that. I'll think of how it's like I'm feeling what you're feeling, which will lead me to conclude that maybe we are all a lot more connected than we think we are in this strange indescribable world.

# Kindness

I'm lying on the floor, arms out to the sides, back on a bolster, head on a folded blanket, in a large room full of light, when it all comes back to me: the snow, the ice, the slip, the fall, the sidewalk bulging before my ground-level eyes. Only appearing to bulge, an optical illusion arising from the sudden onslaught of agony. Because this isn't an earthquake or any other natural disaster, just a private disaster that will go on and on for much longer than I could ever imagine as I sprawled on the sidewalk, getting wet in the recently fallen snow: I thought it was just a dislocated shoulder, I was already planning how I was going to deal with the pain of having it popped back into the socket.

I tried to move but couldn't and my friend Anne crouched beside me looking down, her face full of worry, a little crowd of concerned bystanders gathering around us. Anne going to get her car to take me to the emergency room and a construction worker named Miguel, one of the concerned bystanders, helping me stand up and get into Anne's car according to the instructions of a young EMT worker fetched by his bystander roommate. All of that comes back to me as I lie on the floor in the yoga studio, all of that and more: the emergency room, the dilaudid drip that made the ceiling circle above me like an upside-down sideways merry-go-round, the x-ray of my shoulder where even I could see the broken lines in the shadowy picture. Anne driving me home because Mercy hospital couldn't handle such a complicated orthopedic problem and I would have to go to the University hospital but not then because the University hospital emergency room would be too full on this Saturday afternoon when everyone was slipping and falling on black ice hidden under snow. So they gave me drugs at Mercy and sent me home and Carol and John met Anne and me there.

I remember sitting on my bed with all of them standing beside me, John taking my right hand and lowering me onto the mattress. Later, after Carol and Anne went home, he and I trying to watch something on TV in the living room, telling ourselves that maybe they got it wrong in the hospital and it would turn out to be a dislocated shoulder after all, me drifting off and waking up over and over because of the pain meds, pretending to watch that TV show, pretending to be normal, still thinking I was normal. Later waking up in the middle of the night when the drug wore off, saying John's name because I had to go to the bathroom and I couldn't get off the bed without that steady hand to lift me off the mattress, and him appearing instantly in the doorway. The discomfort I felt about asking him for help. That discomfort wore off slowly, bit by bit, when I had to do it over and over for the next four months, but it never completely went away.

All of that comes back to me as I'm lying on the floor in the yoga studio, on the other side of it all, mostly—as much on the other side of it as I'm probably ever going to get, enough to lie on the floor with my arms out in a yoga class. I feel so grateful to be on the other side of it in this moment that I almost start weeping, and then I think of standing in the lithium water pool in Ojo Caliente hot springs, on vacation in New Mexico with Jo Ann at the end of the summer that year, lithium water pouring from a bronze pipe onto my shoulder and me weeping and weeping although I didn't feel sad at all.

It was as if my shoulder was crying. I could have stood there crying, that water pouring over my shoulder, all day long and not gotten out all of the sorrow that my shoulder was holding. But Jo Ann was sitting in the corner of the pool giving me a look of concern and I didn't want to worry or upset her, couldn't somehow handle her sadness about what she perceived as my sadness, and besides we couldn't sit in that pool all day long. So after a few minutes of crying with the water pouring over my shoulder I got out of the pool and we moved along with our spa day. Which might be why I still feel all this leftover sadness as I lie on the floor in this yoga studio.

What is the epicenter of that sadness? Is it really my shoulder? My shoulder's dismay and sorrow at having been so painfully shattered, its ordinary life disrupted, its ability to function permanently compromised? Is it John? Is it something in my childhood?

I think of John's steady hand lifting me off the bed and helping me lie back down. John standing next to me in the kitchen breathing onto my neck while he tapes Glad Wrap over my bandage so I can take a shower during the first weeks after the surgery. And then me sitting in a rocking chair on Anne's sunporch doing EMDR about three months into the injury, wearing the headset and holding the disks, my shoulder aching, traveling down into my deepest self to root out why I'm so distraught that John has told me in my kitchen that he's moving back East once I'm well enough to be alone. John—this friend that I have loved for many years, who came from D.C. to try out living in Iowa City and ended up staying in my house for the last five months.

I have been so upset about him leaving I couldn't even think about it and now I'm about to get to the heart of why with EMDR: traveling down down down inside myself with the help of the buzzing disks and beeping headphones and landing softly, vaguely, through the magic of EMDR, on the bottom in my earliest childhood: I feel helpless—my body won't work, I can't get up—and then I realize I'm somehow remembering being a baby, that in this vague semi-memory I am a baby and my father is abandoning me the way I feel that John is abandoning me. That's what it is, I realize: I'm having flashbacks to my earliest childhood, being left alone in the house with my terrifying mentally ill mother when my father goes back to work after coming home on his lunch hour to feed me and change my diapers. That John in this broken-shoulder moment is a stand-in for my father all those years ago, in some miracle of synchronicity and healing. Even the details are similar: My father lifting me out of my crib, John lifting me off the bed; my father wrapping a clean dry diaper around me, John wrapping Glad Wrap on my incision to keep it dry when I take a shower. I cry and cry, sitting there on Anne's porch remembering those baby moments of terror of abandonment.

When we stop and I come back up to the everyday world and look around, I realize that my shoulder really hurts and the chair is damp where I've been leaning against it, and then I worry, in my hysterical-at-the-time way, that germs have gotten into the incision and now it will get infected. Because everything scared me then. Standing at the top of the stairs with the possibility of falling. Being driven in a car with the possibility of being crashed into by other cars. (It will be months before I can drive myself and although my shoulder will hurt badly when I do, I will be mostly past the fear of being crashed into by then, mostly beyond the feeling that there are threats all around waiting to injure my injury, even the feeling that it's not quite safe to walk across the ground.)

After the yoga class ends and everyone else has left I stand with Diana, the kind teacher, in the small ante-room off the studio, and tell her about my shoulder, going on and on. I'm sure she's tired and wants to go home but I can't stop telling her about what happened, the details pouring out of me like that water pouring over my shoulder at Ojo Caliente. Every time I think I've reached the end I think of another thing I have to tell her.

How I had to have four-hour shoulder-replacement surgery and they gave me a nerve block before the surgery on top of anesthesia, they didn't even ask me if I wanted the block. How that night in the hospital room the patient on the other side of me kept taking her heart monitor off and the nurses kept turning on the overhead light and tiptoeing past me, the nice one looking over and smiling a little when she saw that I was awake, reattaching that woman's heart monitor and giving her a stern little lecture in hushed voices about how she shouldn't take the monitor off. How John was there earlier that night, bringing me a narcissus in a pot which he had bought in the giftshop, sitting at my bedside till about ten-thirty. At nine-thirty I started panicking because my arm was still dead from the nerve block and I couldn't move it, couldn't breathe, it felt like, and John told me that I could call him any time in the night if I needed to, he would leave his cell phone on. How I couldn't get comfortable after he left, and the nice nurse, Linda, who usually worked in the cardiac department but was in this part of the hospital because she was needed here tonight—by me, I suppose, and that patient who kept taking off her heart monitor—that kind young woman with her bangs and stylish black-rimmed glasses kept coming to my bed to try to make me comfortable. "That looks really hard," she said, moving the pillows, helping me semi-sit up, helping me lie on my side.

At four-thirty in the morning I asked her to help me go to the bathroom. I had to pull my IV stand along with me, and sitting in that little room on the toilet trying to pee—I wasn't drinking water but the IV that was keeping me hydrated made me feel like I had to pee all the time—I thought of MRSA, which I knew they had in that hospital, and how the toilet paper was sitting on the sink counter getting exposed to germs and exposing me to germs when I used it. And I saw where all this was taking me, the broken shoulder leading to the surgery and this night in the hospital leading me to horrible infections leading me to other health problems that would never end.

"I have to call my friend," I said to Linda after she helped me get back to my bed. "Could you bring me my cell phone?"

"You call your friend now?" Linda said.

"I'm freaking out and I have to talk to someone," I told her.

"I'll talk to you," she said. And then she sat down beside me and told me all about how she came to this country from Thailand when she was a teenager, how she broke her foot four years ago and because she was a single mother she had to drive her daughter to school before she was supposed to drive with her broken foot and how hard that was and how hard she knew this was for me, the whole time looking at me with a sweet sympathetic expression. Rather like the look Diana is giving me now as we stand in the anteroom of the yoga studio.

I tell Diana how I had to wear a brace day and night for six weeks after the surgery and Anne made me a cotton sleeve to go between my skin and the unbearable synthetic fabric of the brace's arm and elbow. How I slept in the recliner in my living room for five nights after the surgery, until I started dreaming about being strapped into the electric chair and had to move to my bed and sleep against a huge pile of pillows. How when I woke up every morning, during the month I waited to have the surgery, I felt like one of those eagles with a broken wing in the raptor center, dirty matted shattered feathers hanging off my shoulder, and how every morning after the surgery, for at least six weeks, I was greeted by a sharp-pain reminder when I tried to stretch my arms before I was fully awake. How one night when I was in too much pain John came into my room and sat on my bed and read me an essay by Emmet Fox, and how my friend Jenny Wolffe, the best body worker in the Midwest, came over many evenings, knelt beside my shoulder on the bed, and did what she could to create movement and circulation. How my friend Kris made me cherry cakes and roasted chickens and other friends brought food on other nights according to a schedule they created.

When I finish telling Diana all of that, when I finally run out of things to say and energy to say it, she asks me to show her how far I can lift my arm and whether I can do some other things. She says I'm strong and that my recovery is amazing. I pull my shirt-neck aside and show her my surgical scar. I let the shirt fall back in place and point to the spot on my shoulder where the artificial ball joint sticks out, round and hard, just a little, in the reverse of how a regular shoulder joint goes. She touches that spot, and then she bends forward and kisses it. It's a light simple little kiss, nothing unusual or embarrassing or more than it is, just a small generous act of kindness.

# In the Denver Airport

There are four United customer service representatives behind the desk by the time we get to the front of the line. We've been standing in this line for at least two hours, inching forward so incrementally it's hardly noticeable, and the line stretches out of sight behind us, getting longer all the time. Everyone's tired, babies are crying, people are on their cell phones cancelling reservations at hotels and car rental places in their destinations.

At one point there were only two customer service representatives behind the desk, I learned from my new friend, a young woman who's trying to get to Phoenix, when she came back after doing a little reconnaissance. We started talking a while ago when I told her my cell phone was almost out of battery and I had stupidly packed the charger in the suitcase I decided to check at the last minute and she offered to loan me her charger and I took her up on it. So at least now my phone is plugged into an outlet in a stainless-steel post on the wall. I don't have any contact lens solution with me either and I've been traveling most of the day after having insomnia last night and I'm hungry and my body is protesting after standing in line for so long. But somehow it hasn't occurred to me yet to feel angry, at least not as angry as most of the people around me. Everyone's furious at United Airlines, complaining loudly to their loved ones on their cell phones, yelling at the woman making her way down the line giving us all business cards with the United 800 number on it.  I wouldn't be surprised if someone whipped out a gun and started shooting.

We're here because of an act of God, the card-handing-out woman told the person behind us, so they won't be reimbursing anyone for their ticket or putting anyone up in a hotel overnight. The airport was closed for an hour because one of the towers was hit by lightning during a thunderstorm that came through Denver a while ago and many flights are delayed. All of tonight's flights to Phoenix are cancelled because there's torrential rain there, and my flight, to Santa Fe, has been cancelled too, for reasons nobody told me. "They never close the Denver airport, not even in a big snowstorm," the woman behind me said angrily to the employee who was handing out the business cards with the 800 number, and the employee, no slouch in the anger department herself, snapped back, "You weren't here during that lightning storm."

I'm amazed by how unhelpful and unapologetic the United people are. It's starting to dawn on me that there's no one here who will offer anything in the way of help to me, except maybe the young woman beside me in line, whose name I can't remember. I ask her if she wants to share a hotel room and she says maybe, but she's probably going to drive home, it's an hour and a half in the dark through the mountains and her parents have told her not to but she thinks she's going to anyway if she can get her suitcase back. I'm a little relieved, because while this means I'll have to make my way to some hotel all by myself, I'm also a little nervous about sharing a room with a total stranger. It hasn't occurred to me yet that there won't be any hotel rooms.

Now that we're finally at the front of the line we still have to stand here waiting for a good twenty minutes while the four customer service representatives help other people. "Should we bet on which one will be available first," the guy behind us says. He's a thirty-something German man with wire-rimmed glasses and disheveled sandy hair; he flew here from Stuttgart and is trying to get to a conference in Phoenix. He says he owns his own software company and I tell him I own my own little teeny-weeny business and he says, "What does this mean, teeny-weeny?"

I get the customer service representative I wanted, a young woman with long brown hair and glasses, although this was not who I betted would open up first. She tells me that there's no point in being on standby to Santa Fe tomorrow because there are already ten people ahead of me and there aren't many seats on the plane. There's a 7:55 a.m. flight to Albuquerque and then another one at 12:30. The 7:55 flight is limited too—she holds her hands six inches apart to show me how small the plane is—and already has a long list of people on standby, but the 12:30 flight is a bigger plane and there's only one person standing by for that. So I tell her to put me on standby for the later flight, thinking I'm going to be going to a hotel and will not want to try to make it back to the airport to be ready to board the 7:55 flight which I won't get on anyway.

I stagger off to find a seat somewhere and call the number on a pink slip the customer service representative gave me, which promises to help you find a place to stay overnight at a reduced rate if you're stranded in the airport, but the woman I reach after many rings tells me curtly there's nothing available. The customer service representative told me that the hotel attached to the airport was the Westin and I call the 800 number for that which I find on my twenty-four-percent-charged cell phone. The guy who answers tells me that it will be $315 for a room in the Westin near the airport and I hesitate, then decide to go for it. But then the guy searches and sees that there are no rooms available there, and then he searches his data base for some room that would be available anywhere within twenty miles of the airport and finds nothing. "What's going on in Denver?" he asks in an awestruck voice.

I send a text to Jude, the person I'm traveling to work with for a week as part of my teeny-weeny writing coaching business, then get up and start wandering through the airport looking for something to eat. But there is nothing to eat. Chick-fil-a, the last fast-food restaurant to be open, closes its metal gate as I approach. I wander more and find a place that appears to be open; they have chef salads in plastic containers in a cooler near the doorway and I pick one up and try to buy it but the only employee in sight tells me he's sorry but he has cashed out and has no way to take money or give change. I can see that he is truly sorry but by now I'm finally angry and his apparent desire to be helpful without actually helping makes me angrier. I have half a piece of soggy gluten-free bread and a few shopworn nuts in a Ziplok baggy in my tote bag. The prospect of eating that stuff and nothing else makes me feel a bit like gagging, but at the same time I'm grateful I have it with me because if I didn't I'd be too hungry to sleep.

I stumble back out to the airport thoroughfare and drift along in a daze. There are other people milling around looking stunned and hungry too but not as many as you might think and I wonder if everyone else has gotten a hotel room and that's why the hotels are all filled up. If I had a room it would give me someplace to go and something to do right now. Instead I'm lost in a kind of no man's land, rootless, untethered, not even a bed to sleep in or a case for storing my contact lenses. I think of refugees, of those people stuck in church basements after Katrina, of people who've lost their homes in Afghanistan and Syria and Puerto Rico and many other places—of how although we don't know it, we're all, even us spoiled Americans, just one disaster away from becoming untethered from everything we take for granted.

I find the gate for the 12:30 flight to Albuquerque on the display, shoulder my bag, and start wandering toward the gate. There's no reason in the world for me to be there for another twelve hours at least. But I feel an overwhelming need to find some spot where I should be, which is as close as I can get in this huge echoing anonymous space, to someplace where I belong. I'm filled with an overwhelming sense of displacement—displacement as in having no place—and it occurs to me that the need to have some physical location in the world where you belong, some place which is differentiated from all the other places where you don't belong, is a human drive almost as strong as the need for meaning or purpose or love.

I walk and walk and finally I come to my little patch of temporary home. There's a crowd of people seated at the gate but across from it is a gate that's empty except for two men, one a tall guy with black hair who appears to be working behind the desk. I wait for him to finish talking to the other guy and then I ask him if it's okay to lie down along the wall beside the windows. He looks at me kindly and says, "Wherever you can find." And then he tells me he might have a blanket. He opens a drawer behind him and starts rifling through it. There are two round pillows, the kind you wear around your neck on the airplane, and I say I'll take one of those. He pulls out a yellow rain slicker, says it must've been left behind by someone, and puts it back. "Oh look, a blanket," he says, and hands me a little package with a tiny navy-blue blanket inside.

I lower myself onto a spot beside the window, put the squishy neck pillow under my protesting hips, squash my cloth tote bag into a lumpy pillow and lay my head on it. Someone gave me two Xanaxes a couple of weeks ago in case I had insomnia when I was teaching. I didn't, and I brought them with me in my pocket in case of serious turbulence on the plane. I sit up and fish one out now and swallow it, put my head back down on the lump-filled pillow, and eventually fall into a drug-induced sleep.

I wake up at two-thirty. I'm cold despite my thin blue blanket. There are other people lying on the floor nearby and a few sitting in chairs.

I go to the desk at the gate and open that drawer in the wall where the airline worker found the blanket and the pillow. A little crowd surrounds me instantly and starts rifling through the drawer too. I take out the yellow rain slicker and a woman finds a pillow and someone else searches for a blanket like mine but doesn't find one. I put on the yellow rain slicker; it's way too big and feels cold and greasy but I immediately feel warmer. I lie back down in my spot, swallow the second Xanax and wait for it to take effect, staring out the window at the foggy yellow halide lights and empty baggage carts and other deserted-looking airport jumble.

The view and the moment couldn't be bleaker, and I'm reminded of another time when I was in a gate in an airport, back in the early 1980s when I lived in Boston and I had to fly to New York and give a little sales presentation and I had a phobia of flying and phobia of public speaking. I think of that fear of flying class I took, how they made us to go Logan airport at night and stare through the window at the planes landing and taking off as a means of desensitization; a week later we were supposed to actually fly on a plane but I quit the class before it came to that. I'm not afraid of flying anymore and I don't really understand why I was afraid of it back then. I knew of course that the airplane is essentially a safe means of conveyance. I knew that other people flew safely in them all the time and I knew that I was not so very different from other people, at least not so different that the laws of aerodynamics wouldn't operate in my case. But nevertheless I also knew—in some alternative interior universe with a physics all its own, some irrational subterranean place inside me—that no plane I was on could rise into the air and stay off the ground.

What was that about, I think now as I lie grounded on the floor in the Denver airport. I grew up in a tiny rural New England town where people never went anywhere, either literally and figuratively—they got married after high school, built houses near their parents' houses, had children, became dental hygienists and auto body mechanics. Somehow I always knew I would never have a life like that, but the expectation that I would was imprinted like a template on my inner self. And so were the beliefs and fears and hang-ups that I absorbed from my father, who was worldly enough and had a genius IQ but chose to work in a toothbrush factory, who despised and distrusted cities and travel of any kind. I adored my father when I was a kid. I needed him to rescue me from my mother, I was merged with him in a certain psychic way, and maybe that's why I set up flying in my own mind as something I could never do and which would therefore hold me back. Maybe the fear grew out of some deep unconscious belief that it wasn't safe to be different from him and therefore I couldn't, shouldn't, get off the ground in my life.

I fall asleep again thinking about all that. When I wake up at five in the morning my first thought is to regret not insisting I be put on standby for the 7:55 flight to Albuquerque. I get up, brush myself off, shoulder my bag, and start wandering down the airport thoroughfare looking for something to eat. There's a customer service sign up ahead with a long snaking line of people waiting to be helped by the three customer service representatives behind the desks. I decide to get in line and ask to be put on standby for the early morning flight, but just as I arrive someone pulls a little gate across the end of the line. "These people have been working all night long," they say to a few protestors, "they need to go home."

A woman with glasses and short dark hair comes out from the back. I approach her and show her my standby boarding pass for the 12:30 flight and tell her I'd like to be put on standby for the 7:55 one. She frowns and says that should have been done before and tells me she'll be right back. I wait for a good ten minutes, happy to be being helped and too tired and woozy to care how long she takes. Finally she comes back and hands me a boarding pass that says I'm on standby for the 7:55 a.m. flight. There are at least ten other people waiting to get on the flight, but she's put my name at the top of the list.

When I get to the gate they call my name right away and tell me I made it onto the flight. I text Jude what's happening and she texts me back that she and her husband will pick me up in Albuquerque in an hour and a half. The plane boards, I get on, take my seat beside the window. I feel totally exhausted but calm and cheerful. I wonder briefly whether my long ordeal in the airport will cause a resurgence of my old fear of flying, then decide it won't—in fact, it's just the opposite. Somehow I feel stronger rather than weaker, having gone through one of the worst experiences you can have with air travel, short of dying in a plane crash, and come out the other end.

Pretty soon the plane taxis down the runway and takes off. I put the squishy neck pillow behind my head and promptly fall asleep. I sleep deeply for about twenty minutes, the first time I've ever done that on a plane. Then I wake up and look out the window. Everything is blue out there, there's layer after layer of blue all the way out to the horizon. The sky is a blaze of blue; the towering clouds are tinged with blue; even the ground, an empty plain of mesas and peaked bluffs like waves in the ocean, is a steely grayish blue with a scribble of pink here and there.

Suddenly a memory arrives in me from out of nowhere: It's 1991 and my fiancé has committed suicide and my life has shrunk to the tiniest of pinpoints.  My friend Kathy has driven me from Iowa to North Carolina and she and I are in a film studio where her husband is working as a soundman. And I realize, like a person seeing something for the first time out of the corner of their eye, that if only my fiancé had come here, if only he had remembered all the places you can go and all the things you can do in the world, he wouldn't have killed himself.  I remember that in this moment on this airplane, and I see myself again during that time in the '80s when I was afraid of flying and speaking in front of others, when I couldn't go anywhere or do anything.  All that rushes through me as the plane rushes through the air; something inside me opens up and a wild sense of freedom rushes in, and I think, not for the first time, of how wide the world is, how full of possibilities.

# Acknowledgments

Many thanks to Diane Frank at Blue Light Press for helping this book make it into the world, to Melanie Gendron for her fantastic cover and design, and to Louise Crawford, Edward Velendria, Linda Quigley, and Emma Considine at Brooklyn Social Media, for their invaluable advice, assistance, and support in helping this book find its way.

I'd like to thank all the friends who made it possible for me to generate the material that turned into these essays, by doing 'fast writing' with me, and by reading, praising, commenting, and supporting me in the writing over a long stretch of time, including Mary Beth Shaffer, Jo Ann Beard, Kris Vervaecke, Nina Sernaker, Rita Waggoner, Joe Blair, John Killoran, and Jude Ford. Thanks to all the friends I couldn't possibly live without, including everyone above and John Riley, Heidi Zahner, Dave Rogers, Tania Pryputniewicz, Jeannette Miyamoto, Nancy Ronquillo, Holly Maurer-Klein, Jenny Wolffe, Ann Sinsheimer, Quinn Dilkes, Jill Levin, Lena Tichy, Bruce Grady, Bruce March, and Patty MacInnes. Special thanks to my long-time writing accomplice Jo Ann Beard, my friend and mentor Honor Moore, my partner in healing Anne Cremer, my close friend Kathy Sheldon, my fellow traveler in recovery Carol Edberg, my therapist Alison Milburn, my sister-friend Kris Vervaecke, and my niece Leonika Allen. I'm especially

234 The Deep Limitless Air

grateful to Ruth Allen, Anne Cremer, and Richard Chamberlain for their generous financial help when I really needed it.

"At the Monastery" and "The Deep Limitless Air" were previously published in Tiferet.

"Cowboy Justice" appeared in the anthology, "If I Don't Make It, I Love You: Survivors in the Aftermath of School Shootings," published by Skyhorse Publishing, and on the Little Village website.

# About the Author

**Mary Allen** is the author of *The Rooms of Heaven*, published by Alfred A. Knopf and Vintage Books. She received a National Endowment for the Arts grant in 2002. Her work has appeared in *Poets & Writers, Tiferet, Real Simple, Library Journal,* CNN On-line, *The Chaos, Shenandoah, Spoon River Poetry Review,* and in the anthology *If I Don't Make It, I Love You: Survivors in the Aftermath of School Shootings.* She has an MFA from the Iowa Writers' Workshop and has taught at the University of Iowa. She lives in Iowa City and is a full-time writing coach.

CPSIA information can be obtained
at www.ICGtesting.com
Printed in the USA
LVHW031249250522
719693LV00003B/289